D0418457

THE
FRIENDSHIP
MAZE

THE FRIENDSHIP MAZE

Copyright © Tanith Carey, 2019

All rights reserved.

No part of this book may be reproduced by any means, nor transmitted, nor translated into a machine language, without the written permission of the publishers.

Tanith Carey has asserted her right to be identified as the author of this work in accordance with sections 77 and 78 of the Copyright, Designs and Patents Act 1988.

Condition of Sale
This book is sold subject to the condition that it shall not, by way of trade or otherwise, be lent, resold, hired out or otherwise circulated in any form of binding or cover other than that in which it is published and without a similar condition including this condition being imposed on the subsequent purchaser.

An Hachette UK Company
www.hachette.co.uk

Vie Books, an imprint of Summersdale Publishers Ltd
Part of Octopus Publishing Group Limited
Carmelite House
50 Victoria Embankment
LONDON
EC4Y 0DZ
UK

www.summersdale.com

Printed and bound by CPI Group (UK) Ltd, Croydon, CR0 4YY

ISBN: 978-1-78685-495-7

Substantial discounts on bulk quantities of Summersdale books are available to corporations, professional associations and other organisations. For details contact general enquiries: telephone: +44 (0) 1243 771107 or email: enquiries@summersdale.com.

THE FRIENDSHIP MAZE

How to Help **Your Child** Navigate Their Way to **Positive** and **Happier Friendships**

Tanith Carey

Author of the bestselling
Girls Uninterrupted

Tanith Carey writes on the most pressing challenges facing today's parents. Her nine previous books have been translated into 15 languages, including German, French, Arabic, Chinese, Korean and Turkish, with editions published in the US. Tanith also writes on parenting for the world's leading newspapers including *The Daily Telegraph*, *The Guardian*, the *Daily Mail*, *The Sydney Morning Herald* and the *New York Post*. Tanith is mother to two daughters, aged 16 and 13.

CONTENTS

INTRODUCTION

Every morning, when we say goodbye to our children and send them off to school, we set them off on an extraordinary social journey. Mostly our well-meaning wishes for them to 'Have a good day' are only half heard. We won't have even kissed them goodbye before their focus has turned towards the mini-society on the other side of the school gates.

Concern about homework, tests, and forgotten sports kits pale into insignificance compared to the anticipation of another day: Where are their friends? Who will be there? What will happen at break time? Who will they sit with at lunch? As usual, the school day is likely to bring touching acts of loyalty and kindness, but also devastating acts of rejection and betrayal.

Friendship brings our children both their greatest highs – and their lowest lows. Having a circle of pals who they can be themselves with is the single most important factor in making young people feel good about themselves and want to go to school, according to a wide range of research. Having confidants within their age group gives children the armour they need to withstand the various knocks of childhood, whether it's tension with parents or academic rough spots. Close friendships not only boost a child's self-worth and confidence but they also help them build all the skills they need for healthy adult relationships, ranging from empathy and compromise to how to make up after a row.

As young people start to edge away from their parents towards independence, friends help them define themselves. Friendships matter so much to children because friends find each other. Kids create and care for these relationships all by themselves. In a world where adults tell them what to do most of the time, friends are a choice they make on their own.

Yet despite being such a huge part of their lives, friendship is also the area of children's lives that adults understand the least, and feel the most powerless to help with when things go wrong. When our child comes home upset and tells us they had no one to play with, or they have been left off a party guest list, we feel the lift-shaft plunge in our stomachs as if it were happening to us. Then all too often our protectiveness and confusion lead us to being flooded with conflicting feelings. Why would any child want to be mean to ours? Are they being bullied? Should we intervene and ring the other child's parents? Are we worrying too much?

Yet while childhood friendships have always had their ups and downs, in recent years there have been changes in the way we interact which have made them even more difficult to navigate. Super-powerful phones, which are really mini-computers, have given our young people round-the-clock access to social networks, and dramatically increased the amount of time children spend connected, without being face to face.

On the plus side, this has given young people the chance to have a wider network of different types of 'friends' – many more than we knew when we were growing up.

But the price of extending that circle over social media can sometimes be high. While social networks give them a digital space to chat, and hang out, screens can put a barrier between youngsters which makes it hard for them to judge how they are being received at the other end. As well as the shared jokes and updates, and the photos, remarks can be misinterpreted, 'banter' can cross the line, oblique comments can be taken personally, a lack of likes for a special picture can create anxiety, and an arch remark can quickly escalate into resentment.

There are other pressures that come with social media. These days, to be considered popular, many young people feel they must have a social diary packed with parties and sleepovers, all broadcast in real time on social media.

Every adult remembers the sharp pang they had when they didn't get an invite. As if that was not painful enough, today's youngsters can see their exclusion for themselves, when tiny avatars of their friends show them congregating without them on Snapchat maps, the social media network they use most to talk to one another.

Popularity can now be quantified by numbers of likes, and numbers of friends. Once we never really knew how many friends other people had, or what they were doing after school. Now that information is public. This visibility means that many children feel the pressure to carefully style and edit almost every picture of themselves to win the instant approval of their peers. As one 12-year-old girl told me: 'If you're not getting a like a minute in the first hour when you post a picture on Instagram, you feel like a failure.'

There have been other shifts that have changed the landscape of children's relationships. In our guilt at allowing bullying to become an occupational hazard in schools up until the eighties, we have perhaps now let the pendulum swing too far the other way, and become hyper-vigilant to it. According to many social researchers, the word 'bullying' has come to be misused over the last few years, and applied too casually to describe every hurt, slight and row that is an inevitable part of children's interactions at some time or other.

By the definition of social scientists, however, real bullying is intentional, repetitive abuse by a powerful person towards a less powerful target, and is deliberately meant to hurt and harm. When we are too quick to label everything in this way, the situation becomes oversimplified. One child is immediately cast as the aggressor, the other the victim – when it's not always so black and white.

At the same time, bullying is a word which instantly ratchets up the emotional temperature. It means schools often have to deal with demands from furious parents to punish the child they feel has done theirs wrong – even though trained professionals often find it very hard to unpick who has said what to whom, if the parties are evenly matched. Every child is likely to engage in some bullying behaviour at some point, but that doesn't make them a bully. Tagging them as such means children get instantly demonised, blamed and punished, rather than getting the coaching they need to understand what they have done and how to conduct healthier relationships in the future.

There has been another unintended consequence of our hyper-sensitivity to bullying. Knowing how much trouble they will get in if they are caught, children increasingly adopt a veneer of niceness on the surface, and force their meanness under the radar, behaviour now identified as 'relational aggression'. Name-calling, gossiping, backstabbing, exclusion, ignoring and ganging up are the weapons here. All are deliberately hard to spot. After all, a turned back or a dirty look could all be in the imagination, so children know they are less likely to be caught by adults. Cruel words are as painful to victims as physical blows – and can be more enduring, studies have found.

Many parents worry that meanness also seems to be starting younger. In my interviews for this book, many told me they were dismayed at nasty behaviour already showing up as early as nursery. By four, some children have been found to be using the relational aggression I have just described, to make themselves more socially powerful.

As they grow up, girls in particular are starting their social lives from a position of weakened self-esteem, and between the ages of seven and twenty-one, 69 per cent say they feel they 'are not good enough' according to a 2016 *Girls' Attitude* study. But we also need to remember that these emotions are not just 'a girl thing'. Feelings have no gender. Boys are also suffering a crisis of confidence. More than half of eight to eighteen-year-old boys would now consider changing their diet to improve their looks, and those who feel this way are more likely to feel depressed. Is it any surprise that some children attempt to shore up their fragile self-worth by making themselves feel better at others' expense?

Yet at the same time as callous behaviour is on the rise, several shifts in our education system mean our children are not building the emotional resilience or training they need to stand up to it – and are being deprived of the interpersonal skills they need to resolve conflicts.

At one time playschool was exactly that – a place to play, run around, listen to stories, play dress-up – and also squabble and make up with friends. The amount of free play in our schools is gradually being eroded to make way for the increasing demands of the national curriculum and the SATs tests and to ensure a school's position in the hotly contested league tables. Sadly, by putting them 'on their marks' early, children lose out on the time they need to learn the rules of engagement with others. With less role-play to experiment with their social selves, children get less opportunity to see and swap points of view. With less time to interact within games, they don't get the practice they need to learn how to calibrate the rules so everyone's happy and everyone in the game wants to keep on playing.

All this adds up to a perfect storm in which, according to the latest global data, our children's friendships are suffering the most. Our young people have some of the most fraught social relationships in the world. A 2015 Children's Society report found that, from within the 15 countries they surveyed, England's youngsters are the most likely to say that they had been left out by others in their class at least once in the last month and the England figures are likely to be mirrored throughout the UK. If, as this research shows, these problems are not found to the same extent in every culture, is it time to ask what is going wrong in ours – and what we can do to help make it better for our kids?

The consequences go beyond hurt feelings and broken friendships. If everyday social cruelty is not dealt with, children can also become too distracted to learn and they can also refuse to go to school. Bullying is the fifth most common reason provided for school absence – with 18 per cent of parents giving it as the cause. It is also a common reason parents take children out of mainstream schools and choose home education. Over time, bullying can chip away at a child's self-worth. If it is not addressed, it can contribute to a sense of hopelessness about their lives – and lead to self-harm and suicidal thoughts.

Yet there is hope on the horizon. Just as friendships have come under increasing pressure, the good news is that we have also started to understand these relationships at a deeper level. Until now, parents have believed there is little they could do, from the other side of the school gates, to help children when they get into difficulties. There is now a growing body of research, explained throughout this book, that will help you understand how children really interact. The findings identify patterns and classroom hierarchies in ways that are otherwise hard to put your finger on. As we shall see, by getting an overview, adults can start to crack the code of their children's social lives so we can pass on these insights and help our children make sense of them too.

There is also more help now for the youngsters who find it hard to make and keep friends in the first place. It's long been assumed that some children are just naturally good at forming these bonds, and others aren't. The perception is that youngsters should instinctively know how to form friendships by themselves. However, that idea has been turned on its head by a more up-do-date approach, outlined here too, that shows that if a child finds socialising hard, they can actively be taught the skills to make it easier.

In the same way as children with dyslexia have problems making sense of the jumble of letters they see on the page, social scientists are finding that children who seem to struggle to make friends may have problems decoding and interpreting the social cues they see other people using. While it takes an average person milliseconds to work out those signals, some kids take longer, making them look awkward. In other words, they miss their moment. Considering that psychologists estimate that between 60 and 90 per cent of communication is down to facial expression, body language and tone of voice – rather than what we say – it can leave those children trailing behind. The outcome is that these are the children left on the side-lines, excluded and sometimes bullied. In children's brutal and unforgiving social food chains, many get branded 'losers' or 'weird' – tags they find hard to shake off.

The break-through is that we now know these unwritten rules can be learned and practised. It is still more encouraging to know that research is finding that two of the other key components that draw others to us – a sense of humour and good sharing skills – can also be taught over time.

Overall, this means that if they don't get it by intuition, children can be taught to think about how others see them and to use their eyes, ears and brains to learn what is expected from them.

Resist the temptation to wade in to try and fix all your child's social problems. However, in the same way that you helped them learn how to read or how to behave, you can train them to handle relationships better for themselves. When parents give their children good social coaching they have healthier relationships, more empathy, understand others' perspectives better and are more accepted by their peers.

* * *

To date, almost all of my parenting books have looked at the effect the current environment has on children's mental health. Modern life – with all its conveniences plus all its complications – may be evolving at a breakneck speed. However, our children still need the same things to become emotionally healthy adults, such as close family relationships and good peer bonds. As a parenting journalist, able to talk to a wide range of educators, psychologists and teachers, I have tried to join the dots on the bigger picture. As a mother to two teenage girls myself, I am also in a position to see close-up the subtle shifts in children's social relationships.

After all, the well-being of our children has never seemed like a more urgent issue. According to children's charity Young Minds, one in ten children have a diagnosable mental health disorder – that's roughly three children in every classroom. Half of all mental health problems manifest by the age of fourteen.

Having addressed, in my previous books, how the competitive education system is affecting our children in *Taming the Tiger Parent*, the effect of stress on parents in *Mum Hacks*, and the premature adultification of children in *Girls Uninterrupted*, I felt there was another piece of the puzzle missing – the mounting stress our children feel in their social relationships.

While we adults have more control over our lives, children have much less. Inside the classroom, they cannot pick and choose the people they spend the day with. Even when school is finished for the day, arguments and tension follow them home on social media.

As part of my research, I have not only looked at the body of social science (much of which has not yet been available to parents) to help understand this social world, I have also interviewed teachers, psychologists, school counsellors and, with their parents' permission, children themselves, who were willing to open up about what their relationships are like.

Until now most advice on children's friendships has been aimed at parents with secondary school children – or mostly at girls, but we know now that friendship issues can start as early as four years old, and that boys need help too.

This book is divided into four parts. In the first, I will look in more depth at what has changed in our children's social lives – and what can be done to ease these pressures. In the second, I will summarise some of the latest research about how children's social lives are structured. In part three, I will look at how children who struggle to make friends can be taught to do so and how children can form better friendships. Finally in part four, the book will use the latest research to address some of the most common friendship issues.

You will find that the book switches between talking about primary and secondary school children. That is because the development of friendships is a continuum – and we can't understand our younger children without thinking about where their behaviour may be leading. Nor can we understand our older children if we don't understand where some of the issues they are facing started.

As protective as we may feel, we are never going to be able to help our kids avoid cruel behaviour all the time. Even if we could, it would not be desirable. Whenever humans form groups, there is inevitably conflict. Learning to deal with these flare-ups is an important part of a child's development. As fiercely as we vowed to protect our children when they were newborns in our arms, we cannot shield them from everything. They need to experience some social difficulties. As delightful and perfect as we believe our children to be, at some stage, they will come across other children who don't like them. Inevitably, the time will also come when one of their friends wants to end their friendship – and your child can't be expected to have the perspective to know that this is not the end of the world. That's where we must step in to help give them the bigger picture.

The point of this book is not to shield children from every act of spite or nastiness. It is to help them get through difficult experiences, understand what happened and learn to set boundaries to forge better relationships. Yet at the same time, we must not accept escalating meanness as the norm. When friendship issues flare up for our daughters, we should not dismiss it as inevitable 'girl drama'. When fights and hatred break out in our sons' social relationships, neither should we sweep it under the carpet as 'boys being boys'. Parents tend to think that their sons' friendships are 'easier', but as we shall see they can be every bit as complex as those of girls. Boys, still conditioned to think showing emotion is a sign of weakness, are just better at keeping their feelings under the radar of adults. This may make their social lives look deceptively simple, but we owe it to our boys to be alert for signs they are struggling too, even if they don't demand the same immediate attention.

Week after week, we read new statistics on children's declining mental health – and tragically also stories about some taking their own lives. For our children's well-being – and our own peace of mind – we need to understand our children's social lives better, so we can bring balance and perspective.

First, it will help if we bring an unbiased approach. When our son or daughter's heart gets broken by a friend, we often feel it just as keenly, because it still brings us flashbacks of our own childhood hurts. Reading this book may even unlock some of the reasons why you suffered marginalisation and bullying in your own childhood. Armed with this insight into your own experiences, I hope you can divorce your own from theirs, and help bring more clarity to your advice.

This book can't cover every single scenario your child will encounter, and you can't fix every single problem. There are no magic answers that work for everyone. Some suggestions will apply to your child and others won't. Use this book not as a way to lecture your son or daughter – or to point out that you know better – but as a platform from which to get kids talking. Read out bits to them and see what they think. Use it as a starting point to help them understand the social whirl they are thrown into every day.

At times, making your way through the Friendship Maze – and seeing its twists and turns through the eyes of your child – will be scary. Sometimes, like your child, you will feel utterly dismayed by how complicated and confusing it is. However, with this map in your hands, I hope you will better understand why kids sometimes veer off on the paths they do, and you will develop a clearer idea of how to help them get back on track. However old your child is, set aside any worries that you have not guided them until now. Both parenting and growing up are about trial and error. Now that you have a set of directions, it's never too late to set your child on the right way ahead.

PART ONE
WHAT'S CHANGED IN OUR CHILDREN'S FRIENDSHIPS?

Keely and Livvy have been best friends since Reception class. Every time the teacher asks the children to get into pairs, they don't hesitate for a moment before linking arms. Now ten, they are not sure how their friendship started. They just clicked one day, when they made up a Harry Potter game and found they were both really good at dreaming up fun things for their characters to do together. Together they have travelled through many imaginative worlds. At seven, they would always have a bath together on play-dates so they could make potions out of soap and shampoo. Back then, they hoped this would turn them into mermaids, like it did on their favourite TV programme. The following year they spent every break time making bug shelters on the edge of the playground. From time to time, they had their disagreements – usually over who else to let into their games. Keely and Livvy miss each other too much for their rifts to last long though. The next day, they are back to normal, planning their next sleepover.

Rees is nine and football mad. He loves play-fighting with his two older brothers and his best mate Joe, who he has been friends with since nursery. They are easy and natural together – and nobody makes Rees smile like his best mate. Recently they've moved to the next level by calling each other by their surnames only, to sound as grown up as their big brothers and the footballers they worship. If there's a fall-out in their soccer gang, over a foul or penalty, there might be a quick slanging match between them, but it's forgotten as quickly as it happened.

Whatever the future may bring, these children will always remember these first best friends and how important they were in their formative years. Even if we are no longer in touch with our childhood companions, most of us can still remember the love and loyalty we felt as we explored life together in these early bonds. These special friends were also the people who helped us feel brave as we grew up in the often scary world of school.

As parents, we all desperately want our sons and daughters to have this sort of secure companionship to see them through. At a deeper level, a child's need for friends is about much more than just someone to have fun with. Indeed, a friend feels vital to a child's very survival.

From the moment we arrive in the world, humans are driven to forge social connections. A newborn's initial instincts to connect are so strong that as soon as he opens his eyes, his gaze fixes on his mother's face. Any finger placed in the palm of his hand will be gripped as if for dear life. This innate urge is essential because a baby is completely reliant on the social ties he forms with his first caregivers for food, warmth and protection. Human babies stay with their parents well into their second decade of life, far longer than any animal. Only orangutans – where mothers care for infants for around seven years – come close. During those years, as happens amongst other pack animals, our children will be socialised and slotted into the hierarchies, which always form whenever primates – including humans – group together.

Yet even within the warmth and protection of the pack, alliances are never easy. Scientists have found that friendships are based on reciprocity. In other words, you do something for me and I will return the favour. However, they come with many uncertainties:

- You have to choose another person as a friend, and they have to like you back in the same way.

- As easily as we can enter a friendship, we can leave it – and unlike marriage, it is never made formal.

- There is no on–off switch – which means when you leave a friendship, there is often confusion and hurt feelings.

Our children's need for these bonds may be innate. However, the way our world is changing means that these relationships are becoming more complicated.

Our schools have become bigger, more crowded and more impersonal. The pressure on teachers to produce results and raise league table positions means that there is less playtime for children to interact or practise conflict resolution during the school day. After school extracurricular activities, more screen time and concerns about letting children go and socialise freely with friends, without supervision, means children are given less time to get to know themselves and each other.

No wonder, when we kiss our children goodbye on their first day of school, parents have become more anxious than children. Probably because we know what lies ahead.

Competition – and how it can make childhood a lonely place to be

Molly and her best friends have sat on the top maths table since Reception. Naturally, no one *says* it's the top maths table. It's just called the blue table. But everyone in the class has got the message loud and clear – and Molly and her group want the rest of the class to know it too.

If Molly, a competitive eight-year-old who has been encouraged by her parents to believe she is the best, happens to catch sight of another child working on an easier page in their class workbook, she whispers and giggles to her friends next to her. When the teacher left the room the other day to speak to a colleague, Molly saw her chance – and craned her neck enough to be able to spot the fact that Sophie, on the orange table, was doing a four-times-table worksheet. Molly and her friends had been set work to practise their twelves. Spotting her opportunity, Molly announced: 'I can't believe you're only on that', in front of the rest of the class, causing the other pupils to look round. Sophie fled to the toilet in tears.

Further up the school in Year Six, Luke, Amy and Ethan are among the group also clearly favoured to do well in the upcoming SATs tests. Indeed, the teacher makes no secret of the fact that they are the select, gifted few. Moreover, she believes that setting the group up as an example will motivate the rest. In class, she tells the most gifted group to 'knock [the other pupils'] socks off ' with their correct answers. This has now created a tense atmosphere and a 'them and us' attitude, in what was once a happy and harmonious classroom. When another pupil asked Amy, the most superior of the group, for help during a team exercise, she replied: 'I'm afraid you'll just have to work that out for yourself, won't you?'

And so it goes on in secondary school. In Year Eleven, when the teacher announces that there will be a review of equilateral equations, because some students are not secure with them, Alex, who always sits in the front row, comments loud enough for the rest of the class to hear: 'I can't believe some people still don't get them.'

When children first start school, they are happily unaware of how they compare with their classmates. But, spurred on by a competitive school system, over-arching government pressure for better results and higher placings in the international PISA achievement league tables, it's soon made only too obvious. Parents know more people are competing for fewer jobs – and in their worry, they are putting more pressure on their children to achieve more and to have the 'right friends' to increase their chances of success.

Yet despite our best intentions, when adults pit children in competition against each other, it does not fly over their heads. If we raise them from the start to see life as a contest over everything, from who walks first to who has the most advanced reading book, even small children soon catch on. If the first question we ask them when they come out of the school gates is not 'What did you play at break?' but 'What did everyone else get in the spelling test?', it's no surprise that kids soon learn to measure their achievements not on their own merits, but in comparison to others.

Competition can seep into children's relationships early. Friendships tend to be determined by status. The battle for who is the oldest, most attractive, most socially sophisticated, best dressed or wealthiest starts to organise our classrooms. Often close rivals stick together, not only because they are good matches, but because it pays to keep an eye on their closest opponent as they vie for the top spot. Children will end up pressing each other's buttons, particularly if they are set against each other by their parents, in competition for the same prize. Their social relationships suffer because youngsters learn that it feels good when others fail. Even the video games they play, like *Fortnite*, are about beating others at any cost. By internalising their parents' messages that they must always win, they look for flaws in others and wage an ongoing point-scoring system. The message they get is that they should step over one another to get to the top. To feel like they are pleasing adults, they criticise others to make themselves look better.

As children move up the school, competitive classrooms can become unhappy places, split into cliques. By secondary school, competition moves into different arenas like who is the best dressed, the most socially influential, and who gets the most likes and followers on social media.

Of course, when a parent encourages their child to do well, they are doing it from of a place of love, believing they are arming them with the skills they need to do well in the future. But training our children to treat every classmate as a potential adversary can make the world a lonely place to grow up in.

Australian social researcher Maggie Hamilton observes that teenage girls who feel they have to compete and conform in a competitive world can become hyper-vigilant to threat from any direction – whether it's to their position in the social hierarchy or their spot on the classroom catwalk. Of course, not all children are competitive, but those who are, and who are encouraged to win at any cost, may sacrifice compassion in the process, creating more conflict in their relationships. If they are pushed to achieve too much too soon, they may believe they have to behave like adults before they have had the time to develop a full, emotional awareness of how their young peers think and feel.

It's become a cliché, but we can't afford to lose sight of the fact that it takes a village to raise a child. In other words, it takes an entire community of kind adults looking out for each other's children to produce a kinder society. Studies have found that kids who are raised with a cooperative approach to their peers are likely to be more emotionally resilient, creative and open-minded – all qualities that will be needed more than ever in tomorrow's world. If you support and encourage other people's children, other adults will support and encourage yours. You will also raise children who are kinder to each other.

HOW TO HELP

- **Value every quality:** At the end of the day, instead of asking what marks your child got at school, talk about games they played at break, what made them smile or how they supported or helped another child. Be just as thrilled that your child has been picked as a 'playground pal', or sat with someone at lunch who was on their own, as if they got top marks in their science test. Encourage them to see themselves as well-rounded characters who are more than the sum of their achievements on paper. In this way, they will be less likely to get caught up in competitive power plays with other children.

- **Tell them to compete for their personal best**: There is only one person in life who is truly worth beating, and that's themselves. Show your child how far they've personally come in their lives, either because their early scribbles have morphed into carefully crafted drawings, or their first tentative notes on a musical instrument have turned into polished pieces. If they see how far they have come by themselves, they will also see how far they can go – without the need to compare themselves to, or get ahead of, other people.

- **Let them just 'be' together**: Children need time away from adult-directed activities in which they are constantly being evaluated and compared to others. Create opportunities for kids just to spend time with their friends, playing and having fun.

- **Set out to teach kindness**: We live in a high-pressure age where we think it's our job to teach children to get ahead. Reframe your thinking. No success is worth very much if it is not underpinned by emotional balance and well-being.

A major finding of research by The Children's Society is that unselfish people are happier than people who are preoccupied with their own position. Children can start early by sponsoring a child in need or an endangered animal. Let your child pledge their pocket money to a good cause, or give their old toys to the charity shop. It's never too soon to teach a child how good helping others can feel.

THE BOTTOM LINE: *While there's nothing wrong with success, the question is whether it must always be at the expense of other people's. Make it clear to your child that, in order to win, others don't have to fail.*

Why there's no minimum age on meanness

'My daughter has only been in nursery for a year but already she's had comments from other children like: "You're not my best friend any more," and "So-and-so won't let me play with you." Where do they learn that? How at the age of four are they talking about having set friendship groups?'
Natalie, 32, mother-of-one

> '*Last night at bedtime, my son James, who is six, told me that a few of the boys are mean to him. It's like a little gang is coming together and they feel more on the same side if they are all mean to him.*'
>
> **Danah, 35, mother-of-two**

The first time Melissa suspected that times had moved on since she was a little girl was when her four-year-old daughter Imogen came home from a play-date. 'Immy was so upset,' Melissa told me. 'Another girl told her that singing nursery rhymes was babyish. She told her she should be singing pop songs instead.'

Now her daughter is in Year One, and Melissa is more worried about what certain other children might say to her daughter at school than she is about her reading or writing skills. 'There's a dominant group of girls in the class and some of them can be nasty. They've told her that her work is messy. She says they whisper and laugh at her. If she's reading a picture book in the reading area, they'll come over and tell her that they're already on chapter books.'

At this age, boys are just as sensitive to exclusion. Different primary catchment areas meant that Jacqui's seven-year-old son, James, got split up from his best friend Sam. 'To keep them close, his mum and I arranged for them to go to the same camp during the school holidays. Then another boy from Sam's class turned up too and they preferred to play together. They told James to go away and that they didn't want to play with him. Now he's desperately trying to think of ways to win back Sam's attention. Today, he told me he offered Sam the bag of crisps from his packed lunch. It's heart-breaking.'

So why does meanness apparently seem to be starting younger? Is it that increased awareness of the effects of bullying mean we are more sensitive to it – or is there real evidence of a shift in how children are behaving?

Though it's hard to compare with days gone by, when there was less analysis of children's interactions, a study from America's Brigham Young University has found aggression certainly starts sooner than we might have hoped. It found that girls as young as four are already able to use covert means – like excluding others from their games or making strict conditions for friendships – to assert dominance and get a better footing in the social hierarchy. Boys trail a little bit behind, but research also appears to show they use the same tactics younger (although we are more likely to have a blind spot for it, assuming it's a 'girl thing').

To some extent, much of the way children treat each other is to be expected. Children are, by their very nature, manipulative. They are so lacking in autonomy and physical strength and rely on adults for so long, they have to learn to start looking after themselves. As their social relationships become more important around the age of six, they waste no time testing out their influence over others. So as unsettling as it looks from the outside, much of what children are doing is developmentally normal.

Furthermore, in the early stages, this bid for social power is also more obvious to adult eyes. A child of four may put her hands over her ears to show she doesn't want to listen to another child who does not want to play a game by her rules. By eight, she will have learned that if she's seen doing the same by an adult, she's likely to get a stern telling off. She learns to keep behaviour that will be viewed as undesirable out of grown-ups' view.

Yet, over the last few decades, there have also been several shifts in the modern world which appear to be changing the way our children interact.

The most visible is that children are getting gadgets, such as iPads and phones, much younger – a third of pre-school children already have a tablet.

The problem with giving screens to children at an early age is that it swallows up the time they should be spending playing face to face games with their peers. They get less practice in cooperation, role-playing, and turn-taking – all vital friendship skills. The flashing lights and fast-moving graphics can so easily edge out the basic play which children have engaged in naturally, for millennia, to learn about themselves, each other and how they fit into the world.

Into the palms of their small hands, we put powerful phones which allow them to interact in grown-up ways, but away from adult eyes. The average age a child gets their first phone is now ten. Yet at this age, youngsters are still developing the higher thinking parts of their brain, which helps them make good decisions. It means that we are giving them devices which allow them to do or say anything that comes into their heads, before they have learnt to understand fully the impact their words or actions have on others.

Over the last twenty years, the boundaries between adult and child screen entertainment have also blurred. Whereas once youngsters watched after school children's TV at set times between 4 p.m. and 6 p.m. – featuring 'safe' programmes like *Blue Peter* and *The Magic Roundabout*, too many now wander freely on YouTube. Here, *Peppa Pig* videos sit casually alongside home-made clips of seven-year-olds giving make-up tutorials, and dispensing advice about how to be the prettiest girl in the class. For the boys, there are the latest uploaded videos of school fights, and countless expletive-filled, abusive commentary clips of their favourite video games. There are entire video genres comprising of cruel practical jokes, captured on smartphones, and uploaded for maximum humiliation.

As parents, we too have had to adapt to a changing and more competitive world. In an uncertain era in which we worry more about our offspring's future job prospects, even while they are in primary school, there's the creeping tendency to excuse more dominant, controlling behaviour as a promising sign of leadership, feistiness and influential social status, just as long as it isn't seen to cross the line into 'bullying'.

Hyper-vigilant to every threat, many of us feel like our sons and daughters have to grow up to protect themselves at all costs.

Inadvertently, we may find ourselves excusing social manipulation as a life skill. One mother told me how the dominant child in her eight-year-old's friendship group was controlling how the other members dressed, wore their hair and who they could speak to at school. She told me, 'I messaged the mum to suggest we looked at ways to tone it down. The answer I got back made it sound like the mother was impressed by her daughter's leadership skills. She seemed to think the playground was *The Apprentice* and it was a sign her child was going to be a future CEO.'

We now know that how a child behaves socially is formed very early in their lives. Like every part of their development, their friendship skills need to be built step by step. Socialisation should never be rushed. If it is, children miss out on vital lessons they need to help them learn to make and keep good friends.

HOW TO HELP

- **Let children be children**: While it's true that the more socially sophisticated children tend to have more influence in their peer group, it's still important that our children are not encouraged to grow up too fast. Treat them as the age they are and don't delight in them looking or behaving like mini-adults.

- **Start at home**: Even though it may not always feel like it, sisters and brothers, and other family members such as young cousins, are often a child's first friends. They give children the chance to practise sharing and cooperating every day and learn friendship skills early. As they grow up together, train children to see each other's points of view. For example, tell your son about his little sister: 'Kaya has put her hands over her eyes. She doesn't like it when you throw the ball so hard. Try rolling it instead'. Take the time to notice and remark when siblings are sharing with each other and are considerate – and they will turn into better friends.

- **Talk about friendship**: Get them off to a good start by talking about what it means to be a good friend – and help them learn to be cooperative, share and take turns. Use role play games, in which puppets and toys have different perspectives, to show that not everyone thinks the same way they do. Show how it's OK to have disagreements – whether it's over whose turn it is to drive a toy car, or what they plan to do on a sleepover – and how there is usually a way to work around them.

- **Delay screens**: Explain phones are not toys and hold off screens as long as possible. They open up a world which young children are not developmentally ready for. Give your sons and daughters lots of opportunities for free, real-world play and to take part in games which teach them social skills.

Growing older younger – how physically growing up too soon can affect friendship

> 'A lot of girls want to look like the ideal woman or celebrities. It starts very young at primary school. I remember being five when I first wanted to put make-up on to look like celebrities in magazines. The girls who seemed older and wore make-up first also seemed to have more power in primary school.'
> Taylor, 12

With her hair in bunches, Atlanta looked like any other happy-go-lucky eight-year-old in her class picture, taken at the start of Year Three. But as her mother Emma told me, there was much more on her mind than play-dates and her latest favourite book.

She had already started her periods.

'Atlanta was in the bath when I first noticed a few hairs, when she was eight years and three months old,' said Emma, 37.

A few months later, her periods started. Yet, when she consulted her GP, Emma was surprised to hear that Atlanta's hormones were considered to be in the normal range for a child her age.

According to the most recent study by the University of Plymouth, children are reaching puberty five years earlier than a century ago.

In girls, breast development is generally the first sign of adolescence. The most comprehensive research to date suggests that this starts in about 10 per cent of white and Asian girls, 15 per cent of Hispanic girls and 23 per cent of black girls by the age of seven – around double the number fifteen years ago.

Doctors are not clear how to fully explain the phenomenon – but one theory is that exposure to chemicals, which mimic the effects of hormones, and which are in foods as well as plastics, may be triggering puberty sooner. Other studies have linked it to the fact that girls are generally gaining weight, earlier in life. The latest figures from NHS Digital show nearly one in ten children now starting Reception are obese. Increased fat stores in the body in turn increase levels of leptin, a hormone which can bring on menstruation sooner.

It means that some of the children who appear to be growing up faster than ever actually are – and that can have a knock-on effect on their peer group relationships. Even if their periods have not begun, their hormones are starting on a rollercoaster several years before, which can trigger mood swings.

The most physically mature girls tend to be the peer group leaders of their groups. Yet they may achieve these positions before they are mentally ready for them.

In boys, puberty is starting earlier too. According to the biggest scale study to date of 4,000 young males, more boys are also starting to mature between the ages of nine and ten. It means they are starting adolescence up to two years younger than their fathers' generation.

The difficulty for parents with sons is that the early symptoms of puberty are not as visible as in girls. Boys don't show the more obvious traits of male puberty – like facial hair and a deeper voice – until closer to the end of adolescence, say 14 or 15. It means parents may have to work harder than ever to try to understand their sons during this critical moment in their development. As psychologist Nigel Latta explains: 'We know a lot about the physical aspects of puberty, but the psychology of it, particularly for boys, is something we're only just beginning to look at. Part of the difficulty in understanding boys' experience is that their usual response to most questions is "I dunno", or some variation on that.' Latta says parents should realise that young boys experiencing puberty are often not yet emotionally equipped to deal with the testosterone surges that may accompany it. 'The part of their brain which is supposed to help quell the angry moments is still a work in progress. Your job as a parent is to remember they have a limited ability to calm themselves down, and de-escalate things.'

HOW TO HELP

■ **Treat your child as the age they are, not how old they look:** So often, we take more notice of what we see with our eyes than what we know in our heads. Even if a child looks physically developed for their age, emotionally they are still their chronological age. Children may have more adult hormones in their bodies, but their brain development is still lagging behind.

■ **Talk openly:** Although it may be startling for you, be positive about the changes in your child's body so their self-worth doesn't suffer. Avoid referring to the changes puberty brings as negative or something to be ashamed of. Talk about how these developments are preparing them for the future, but let kids know they still have lots of learning and growing up to do.

How the rise of reality TV impacts children's social relationships

'The girls at school talk about "drama" and "beef" as if it's entertainment. There's even a popcorn emoji to use on social media to show the others you're enjoying watching the row.'
Maya, 14

On a Friday afternoon meet-up after school, a group of 12-year-old boys gather around an iPad to watch the latest episode in the life of Jake Paul. While largely unknown to anyone under 20, Jake has woven a complex web of personal drama around himself to help win a fan base of over 11 million for his daily vlogs on YouTube. It's hard to know how much of the emotion behind the rows, insults and disses are made up or exaggerated.

Much of the conflict revolves around his ex-girlfriend, Alissa Violet, his brother, Logan and his other YouTube rivals. This involves various rivals 'dissing' and 'roasting' each other with insulting rap songs, which also rack up tens of thousands of downloads. This is a high-energy world where 'drama' wins you not only a rapt audience of adolescent followers, but also TV contracts, elite sports cars and ad revenue.

Nor are grown-ups setting a better example on reality TV programmes like *Dance Moms* or *Real Housewives* – which children can view any time of the day or night. Here feuds are the main plotlines and arguments often erupt into finger-jabbing confrontations.

Indeed, studies are finding that female aggression on TV is now so common that it is viewed as an inevitable, female character trait. In an analysis of TV programmes, researchers found that the meanest female characters on TV were rewarded for their bad behaviour with attention or material possessions.

There is strong evidence that children mimic behaviour they see onscreen. More than 1,000 pieces of research have drawn a link between TV violence and aggressive behaviour in children. Now the violence is verbal.

A study of more than 1,100 tween and teen girls by the Girl Scouts Research Institute found that girls who regularly watch reality TV, accept and expect more aggression in their lives. Also, the more they watched these shows, the more they measured their worth by how they looked. While adults have the life experience to see through the hype and staged set-ups, children are more likely to believe this is how the world works. Three-quarters of those quizzed believe the shows are mostly real and unscripted.

Here conflict is sold as entertainment – and as something that is part and parcel of relationships. It's seen as a template for how the adult world works – and subconsciously sends a message to children that it's acceptable to behave like this. It seems that girls are more likely to be affected. Studies looking at the links between socially aggressive behaviour and aggressive TV characters found there was no change to boys, but in girls there was a rise.

Australian researcher, Larry Owens, of Australia's Flinders University has found that, as a result, girls aged 15 can find social drama entertaining and sometimes spread rumours to create excitement. As stories spread around the school about, for example, activities at a weekend party, there's great excitement as students eagerly listen and then pass on their own embellished versions of stories to others. The girls treated their own lives like the soaps, hoarding drama, constantly rehashing trivia. Teachers told Owens some girls were 'treating life a little like it was a TV drama.'

It's no wonder when reality TV shows contain an average of 85 verbal attacks, insults and snide remarks each hour – almost twice that of comedies, dramas and soap operas. Research has found that half of these incidents were organised by producers baiting participants into bitching about their rivals.

Yet it's far from harmless entertainment because the cruelty can keep going even after the screens have been switched off.

HOW TO HELP

- **Watch TV with your children:** As adults, we are mature enough to know the difference between real life and the behaviour shown on reality TV. Meanwhile, children generally do not have the life experience to draw a line between what's shown as 'real' on reality TV, and what actually happens in the real world. So if your child wants to see this kind of programming, sit down and watch it with them. Talk about the behaviour they are seeing, whether it's kind or unkind and how you think people should behave to one another.

How being busy affects our children's social skills

'I knew I was on the phone too much for work when my three-year-old son would cry when I started emailing on it and try to grab it out of my hands. Once he tried to flush it down the loo.'
Richard, 51, father-of-three

There's a reason why more primary schools are sticking up signs on their gates saying: 'Put your phones away. Your child is pleased to see you.' While we have been busy worrying about the attraction of children to gadgets, we have become sucked in ourselves.

Of course, there's no denying the huge convenience factor of phones. Yet the creeping tendrils of technology means that they can so easily distract us from the most precious things in our lives – our children. Because of the time we spend checking emails, working, shopping and catching up on our social media feeds, we are now spending less time talking to our kids. As we have had to multi-task more, we have allowed our children to use technology more too. A recent poll by a parenting website found that half of parents routinely allow infants to play with their iPhone or tablet. One in seven allows their tot to spend more than four hours a day playing with their gadget. It's no wonder the term 'iPaddy' has evolved to describe the tantrums sparked when these devices are taken away.

When they see the way their baby's eyes light up at the sight of the flashing screen, it's understandable that parents often hand them over – they're more soothing than dummies. Many parents are also confused because it can seem like this screen time can be justified with educational apps.

However there is still no clear evidence that such software improves learning. Even if there are marginal gains, the time spent on screens takes away from the time young children should spend on areas of their development, such as active, physical play, human interaction and communication.

Indeed, the ages between nought and four is a critical window when children's brains are the most receptive to learning language. They are busy building neural pathways that will be important for the rest of their lives.

The growing amount of time young children spend on touch-screen technology has led to nursery teachers now observing some youngsters lacking the communication skills required to talk to each other and make friends. It means that even a simple question like 'Would you like a glass of water?' leaves some children unable to answer. The knock-on effect is that young children, who cannot make themselves understood, either have outbursts of frustration, or they become quiet and withdrawn as they find communicating so difficult that they stop trying. The other outcome is that some youngsters start school without the skills to make friends. They lack the language to communicate with their peers, take turns, or play the most vital bonding game in early childhood, Let's Pretend.

HOW TO HELP

- **Be your child's first friend**: While the pressures on friendships sounds concerning – and may prompt a good deal of soul-searching among parents – the good news is that it's never too late to improve your child's communication and friendship skills. The change can begin today. By taking steps to limit your phone use, interacting and role-playing with your children more, the effects will be instantaneous. Holding ordinary conversations, playing games, doing simple things together – like cooking and going for walks – are all you need to do. By spending uninterrupted time with your youngsters, they feel liked and loved. That makes them feel likeable to others – and that's always good news for their friendships.

- **Screens are not babysitters**: Screens do keep children transfixed, allowing parents to get on with other stuff, but the price for too much free babysitting is high. Around the world, many experts now recommend that under twos should have as little screen time as possible, except for video-chatting. If that sounds like a tall order, and you do give your child a phone to play with, limit the time to no more than 20 minutes – and be there to play along with them, so you are still chatting and communicating with them. Afterwards, offer a much more interesting alternative – a one-to-one activity with you.

- **Play make-believe**: When your young child asks you to play a game of Let's Pretend, accept their invitation as often as possible. Child development experts say there is no other activity that does more to improve a child's language and social skills in the early stages. Pretend play helps kids better express their emotions in every area of their lives. They will learn to regulate their feelings more readily because they will have learned to articulate how they feel more clearly. Children who have played a lot of cooperative role-play games are more likely to make and keep friends easily, because the interaction has helped them learn to take turns and communicate better.

- **Give them special time**: Give children ten minutes of pure, undivided attention at least once a day throughout their childhoods. For this period, let them be in charge and don't try and teach them anything. Giving your time to play a game of their choosing, whether it's playing shops or drawing with them, will also make them feel loved and valued and help grow their feelings of self-worth. In turn, that will make them feel more confident as they interact with other youngsters.

- **Ring fence your tech use**: When our phones run so much of our lives, it's easy to slip into a pattern of over-using them in front of the children. It's critical your child never feels your phone is more important than they are, so think about how you can be more present and less distracted. Turn off your notifications and use auto-reply more, so you don't feel the need to respond and interrupt your time with them. Flip the lid down on your laptop when they enter the room to show you want to chat. Draw up a list of screen use rules for your home that everyone must abide by. These may include no phones for anyone within an hour of coming home – so you can reconnect and talk about the day – as well as a ban at meals, during family outings or before bedtime, which is another important time to connect.

THE BOTTOM LINE: *The roots of a child's social confidence come from the love and approval they are given by their first care-givers at home. The deeper those roots, the better they will be able to stand up to the inevitable conflicts that will come their way in the wider world.*

Why children need more playtime

Even if you have only the faintest memories, it's likely that you look back on your early school days as some of the most carefree of your lives. Your time was probably spent sitting cross-legged, chanting songs and listening to stories. The rest was whiled away moulding clay, finger-painting or lacing pasta necklaces. The biggest stress was running out to get a turn on the climbing frame or swing. Probably your first very basic sums were learnt playing shopkeepers with grey plastic coins.

These days the nursery 'curriculum' is far less free and easy. Now the talk in pre-schools is of assessment trackers, and learning journeys. Before they have even turned two, toddlers are assigned specific areas of learning and development, including 'literacy' and 'maths'.

In the state sector, playing cafés in the home corner or finger painting are no longer deemed to be enough preparation for life either.

It all starts gently enough, with checks on whether a very young child 'is becoming aware of how to negotiate the space and objects around them', 'can communicate their physical needs for things such as food and drink' or 'can let adults know when they are uncomfortable'.

After that, the pace quickens. There are nearly seventy centrally set 'early learning goals'. By five, children are expected not only to be able to count up to twenty, but also to show that they can solve number problems and understand concepts such as halving and doubling. But then, as one education minister put it, you don't want toddlers 'running around with no sense of purpose'.

As a result, head teachers are continuing to cut break times and playtimes to keep up with curriculum requirements. A report from the Nuffield Foundation found that schools have been cutting break times since 2006.

This comes at a cost. Play has always been mankind's first form of education. All the young of mammals play. The differences between the way that puppies, kittens and baby apes play shows how they practise the skills they need the most. Antelope play at running and dodging, while young tigers practise pouncing and stalking. By taking away play, we take away our children's very survival skills.

Yet, as the pressure from above bears down on the curriculum, teachers increasingly believe that the reason they are seeing more behaviour issues in the classroom, as well as bullying, is that children have less opportunity to work out their issues – and learn how to behave. When children play games, they learn how to compromise, make up rules, think creatively and learn which behaviour is acceptable to others and which is not. You have to imagine scenarios, share ideas and create worlds in which all participants want to belong. Get it wrong and your playmates leave and the fun stops.

HOW TO HELP

- **Give children more time outside**: Children used to have two educations. The one they had at school and the one they had from nature. It was in those moments when we played outdoors, away from adults, that we learnt how to think of ourselves as independent beings, who could make our own decisions, take risks and look after ourselves. The unintended consequence of keeping kids busy indoors – because we feel it's safer for them – and filling their time with adult-directed activities like homework, learning apps and extracurricular, is that we have eroded the downtime they need to work out who they are and the best way to interact with others. When UNICEF asked children their requirements for happiness they named three things – time with families, time outdoors and having friends. All three are intimately related.

  Yet kids rarely get this time. While 73 per cent of seven to twelve-year-olds surf the internet unsupervised, according to a study by Play England, 42 per cent are not allowed to play in their local park without an adult.

Among children aged two to five, 69 per cent can open a web page browser, yet only 20 per cent know how to swim. Fifty-eight per cent can play a computer game, but only 52 per cent know how to ride a bike. For your child's well-being, make time for explorations into nature for your child and your family – whether it's after school, at weekends or during holidays.

- **Teach them new skills:** If you look back to your favourite snapshot memories from your own childhood, there's a good chance you will remember moments of self-discovery when you found out you could do something on your own. But when children do not get a chance to practise this independence, they think it means we have no confidence in their abilities. If you wait on children hand and foot, as you did when they were babies, they tend to believe it's because they are incapable of looking after themselves. Whether it's making an omelette or changing a light bulb, think first about what your growing child is ready to do for themselves – not what you can do for them. You will know they've added another building block to their self-worth, when you see the huge, natural smile on their faces after they've done something all by themselves for the first time. Over the course of a childhood, building up this inner core helps children feel capable, useful and self-sufficient. The unexpected bonus will be that they will grow up more resilient. By helping them build their unique skills, talents and competencies, they will also feel more secure in themselves and have less need to put others down to bolster their self-worth.

How getting on with other parents helps your child's friendships

> 'There's a group of mums in my son's nursery who have deliberately set out to make their boys friends with each other because they have the same sort of homes, cars, holidays and lifestyles. They're not really that interested in play-dates if you have a child outside that group, no matter what happens at playtime. It's the mums who decide, not the children.'
> Nikki, 34, mother-of-one

The stories of bullying – and the suicides linked to them – that keep surfacing on our 24 hour news cycle mean that, as parents, we have understandably become hair-trigger sensitive to even the slightest hint our children are being ostracised. Bullying and friendship problems have also been named as the number one reason for self-harm by nearly 30 per cent of children.

Yet by becoming so hyper-vigilant about our children's social lives – and taking any slights personally – we are doubling the pain in many ways.

We forget the many ups and downs we had during our childhoods, and only remember the sharpest pangs we felt in our darkest hours. When our child is rejected, it's only those most painful memories which return to haunt us, rather than the more casual day-to-day cruelty we managed to endure.

The flip-side of this overprotectiveness is that concerned parents often go on the offensive too soon. When we first start our parenting journey, it's tempting to get over-involved, by imagining we can create a 'safe' social circle by setting up play dates with parents we view as 'people like us'. Yet in the longer term, trying to intervene too much – and engineering our children's relationships – does not make for happy classrooms.

Instead the consequences of trying to build our children's social circles can be the sort of cliquiness at the school gates that makes school life unpleasantly stressful for everyone, whether you are on the inside or the outside. Ultimately, all this does is create a pressured and unfriendly atmosphere amongst parents, which can trickle down to the children. Given that our kids watch our every move and are keen observers of how we interact with others, often these parent hierarchies can start to be mirrored in our children's social structures. By Year Three, most parents will have observed the Queen Bees amongst the mothers and the King Pins amongst the fathers, who will often have children taking up similar positions inside the school gates.

Ultimately, standing up to these pressures – and letting your son and daughter pick their own mates – will give your child more meaningful bonds which stand a higher chance of success.

HOW TO HELP

- **Respect your child's likes**: Be honest. Are there some children you'd rather your son or daughter were friends with than others because of their social status or family background? For better friendships, let your child decide. Be equally enthusiastic about inviting any child your son or daughter plays with at school, whether you like the look of their family or not. As child psychologist

Dr Michael Thompson points out in his book: *Mom, They're Teasing Me*, 'A school that has a problem with cliques among students often has problems with cliques among the parents as well...'

- **Avoid party one-upmanship**: It can be helpful to remember that a children's party should not be a message to the other parents that you are the 'best parent'. Being the 'best parent' is actually about listening to and connecting with how your child wants to celebrate.

- **Be open:** Having a good group of parent friends who can provide support and help as your child moves up through school is great. Ignoring the other parents outside the group – or not inviting their children for play-dates – is not. Be prepared to talk to every parent in your child's class, not just the ones you feel you have a lot in common with. Every human being deserves to be treated with basic courtesy, no matter who they are. By role-modelling this for your child, you will be passing on one of the most important life lessons there is.

- **Get to know all the parents of children in your class:** At first it can look daunting to penetrate groups who look like they all know each other in the playground. Suggest setting up a WhatsApp or Facebook group, not only to support each other and set up play-dates, but also to get a better idea of who the kinder parents are. They are also more likely to have kinder kids.

How social media has changed friendships

'I went through a phase when I had really bad skin. It really hurt when some of the nastiest comments on my pictures came from a group of people who I thought were mates. They saw it as banter but they never said it to my face. I tried to take it on the chin, but actually it made me feel like less of a person.'
Jacob, 15

'Your so annoying u broke uw [UP WITH] my friend u cheat b*tch.'

'Id [I DON'T] think anyone likes you freak. your ugly and a b*tch.'

'You are a d*ck I hope u F*****G die you f**k boy. Go slit your wrists.'

Messages between an 11-year-old boy and girl

'I'm really upset; the other day my friend showed me some horrible pictures that people were posting on Instagram of me. Some people put silly tags on pictures of hippos and put my face on them. I think my parents know something is wrong but I really don't want to talk to them about it. I am so embarrassed to tell them. I can't seem to get away from it and everyone else can see it too.'
Alannya, 13

'You see it happening to other people first. Sarcastic comments next to photos like "Love your outfit" or "You're so pretty". Most of the time you're a bystander and you don't say anything because you don't want those people to turn on you.'
Jade, 16

'I can't say I don't enjoy social media, but I do see it causes problems, especially among the girls.'
Chris, 15

At first glance, it appears to be any ordinary play-date for two primary schoolgirls.

In a pink-walled bedroom, decorated with posters of Justin Bieber, best friends Zoe and Eleanor settle themselves onto the bed and prepare to press play on camera phones.

'This is mine and Eleanor's hot-or-not video', announces Zoe, waving two sheets of A4 covered with names of her school-mates. 'If you're on it and we say you are not pretty or good looking, don't get offended', pipes up Eleanor, issuing the standard disclaimer for videos of this kind. 'It's just our opinion!'

The roll-call then begins. 'Cerys Thomas' is the first of the 30 names on the list to be read out register style. 'Hot!' the girls immediately exclaim in unison. Next is 'Lianne Simons'. 'Hot!' is the decree.

The name of a third classmate, however, is met with a pause just long enough for the girls, aged no more than 10 or 11, to exchange knowing smirks.

'Not hot – sorry!' they chime in small, high voices, which belie the cruelty of what they are saying.

In all, seven more classmates, both boys and girls, get the thumbs-down. As soon as the last judgement is handed down, the girls sign off with a satisfied 'Thanks for watching!' – so easy when you can't see the stricken faces of the classmates you have just publicly humiliated.

When the video is uploaded to YouTube, the clip gets 120 views in a matter of days, making it clear that no one in their class – or perhaps their primary school year – will have missed it.

The format of these 'hot or not' videos is standard. They are filmed mostly by girls, some of whom look no older than nine, both alone or with their best friends, in their bedrooms. Verdicts on their sophisticated ranking system are delivered within singsong tones – but with the brutal certainty of high court judges. They behave as if they are performing an invaluable service by letting their peers know where they come in the school looks hierarchy.

Yet even though so many of these videos seemed to be filmed at bedtime, these children seem to inhabit an entirely adult-free zone. By secondary school, young people justify these clips on the grounds classmates can put themselves forward to be rated, by 'liking' a status announcement, when they hear someone at their school is planning to film one.

Popularity and good looks have long been prized in adolescence. But a generation ago, it was not pointed out on social media if you did not score highly in these counts. Already plagued by the insecurities of puberty, today's children feel they must measure up to impossibly high ideals of looks and bodily perfection on photo-sharing sites like Instagram and Snapchat, as well as dress themselves according to a red-carpet-ready dress code if they want peer group recognition.

Unlike real life, here images are more malleable with filters, flattering angles and retouching. At first, it gives young people the illusion of control. Here they hope they can project a glossy image that will give them the status they dream of as a mini-celebrity, for which you must have a minimum of 500 followers, even if your profile is on private and not public mode.

All too often, it's the most insecure youngsters, who are the most unsure of their place on the classroom catwalk, who put themselves forward to seek the validation they won't get.

When they don't get the approval they crave, the least successful put themselves up for online contests, like 'Who's the prettiest?' or 'Who would you date?' Here they volunteer to put their eager young faces onto a grid, where they are put to the vote. As they get voted out, their faces are automatically scratched out in this brutal game of noughts and crosses.

Here, being 'fit' is what's needed to win the highest form of praise, which is either 'peng' or 'queen' for girls. The ultimate accolade in the comments is: 'You slay my life'. For boys, clips of skateboarding tricks and shots of their abs, sharpening jawlines and £200 trainers are offered up in the hope of being called 'roadman', 'legend' or 'king'.

Conveniently, these images mainly speak for themselves. The selfies at the parties and the group hugs at get-togethers, dripping with the 'you had to be there' in-jokes help to build the walls of friendship groups even higher.

For girls who are already socialised to compete for attention, and are more wired to think about what others think about them, Instagram and Snapchat can be almost impossible to stay away from – and can occupy a huge chunk of time and headspace. Research shows that boys, showing off six-packs and 'on fleek' (perfect hair-cuts) – are catching up fast.

And behind the silly faces, the goofy poses and the hugs, there are often social wars being played out. Cliques of friends guard their circles by giving themselves names, like Ace Gang, Squad and others based on inside jokes. Like Masonic symbols, the particular emoticons used next to members' bios are for clique use only.

All this quickly falls apart in a fight, when it becomes a race to see who's going to block who first – and then to message your friends to block your enemy too, followed by text recriminations all round.

Social media makes staying in touch with their friends – and celebrating the fun they have with them – incredibly easy. But it also makes settling scores – and expressing resentment – easy too. It takes just a moment to add an ambivalent comment next to a picture, or post a video in which everyone knows who is being talked about, even if the person is not named, to kick-start a row.

Indeed it might be virtually invisible to the naked eye.

A group of friends might post a group picture and intentionally not tag your daughter in it. The following day, she may be left off a group message, then, the girl she thought was her best friend may tag someone else as her best friend. A friend who might normally have been expected to compliment a photograph says nothing.

When 'beef' or 'drama' does finally blow up, it is not only witnessed by a child's close circle, but by dozens of people in their year group, many of whom view their discomfort and upset as entertainment.

The next day the online tension is likely to manifest in the real world – and the sarcastic emoticons, check-mate style blocking and oblique comments are replaced in 3D, for girls in particular, by ignoring, glaring, conspiratorial whispering and turned backs in the classroom and lunch hall.

Then there is the sheer hard work for young people of monitoring their online social lives. If you've ever just prised a phone from a tween's hands, you may be amazed by the relentless number of blips, chimes and shudders it makes as more notifications flood in. Scientists say this cognitive overload increases stress hormones in the brain – and it seems to be one of the reasons that our children are more anxious than they once were.

However, talking to young people, there are some positive signs that, because they grow up seeing cruel remarks as a fact of life, they are becoming more resilient.

But this toughness can be hard-won, and, as parents, we cannot afford to underestimate the painful ripple effects of a cutting remark at a vulnerable time.

HOW TO HELP

- **Monitor social media:** Many parents still don't keep an eye on their child's online activities, thinking it's an invasion of privacy. Yet learner drivers aren't allowed into other public open spaces without an instructor and dual controls. Until they are ready to go it alone, you should be there to help your child negotiate the twists and turns, and, if needs be, apply some brakes before a situation veers out of control. Knowing they have a parent near will also make your child more likely to think again about posting something irresponsible or mean. From the outset, make it a condition that you are a 'friend' or 'follower' on your child's social media accounts, until you feel they have really learned enough for you to allow them to go it alone. However, even if you monitor their social media, be aware that much of the interaction will be so subtle that it will pass under your radar. So foster a relationship in which you can ask your child to talk you through it. At relaxed times, take an interest. To help you understand, ask them to scroll through their feed. Contrary to what you might think, if you are calm and uncritical, researchers have found youngsters enjoy sharing what's happening on their social media feeds with their parents.

- **Keep it in perspective for them:** Being popular has always been important to young people, never more so than when they see solid proof of their status in comments, likes and shares. Help them keep a sense of proportion though. Robert Faris, an associate professor of sociology at the University of California says small tweaks and changes in attitude can make a difference over time. 'Encourage them to try not to keep score. Don't sweat the small stuff. Don't worry if you're not tagged. Don't count likes. Don't exclude other people.'

- **Make it a condition not to swap passwords:** Passwords are often exchanged as tokens of loyalty between friends – or so they can share social media accounts. If a relationship sours, embarrassing or inflammatory comments could be posted in your child's name. Tell them that passwords are private property and to let their friends know that you make it a condition of their phone use. The only people who know them are your child – and you.

- **Talk to your child about location and anonymous apps**: To adults, it may seem like madness for youngsters to allow people to make anonymous comments about them. But there are a range of features that they can add to Instagram profiles allowing people to make comments and ask questions without being identified. Unsure of who they are or what others think of them, a surprising number of children use them. However, this cover of anonymity can give their peers the heady feeling that they are not accountable at all for what they say. Instead of a message from the boy or girl they secretly hope likes them, or expressions of admiration, all too often youngsters get cruel messages from others who are being mean because they can be.

- **Help them do the right thing**: You won't be there when your child is engaged in an online row, but if they know and understand your values, they will have internalised your guidance in their mind and that will help them make better decisions. For example, when they are on social media, and they hear the inner voice of common sense telling them: 'Maybe posting this isn't such a good idea', ask them to listen out and pay attention to it. If the thought: 'They deserve it', also pops up before they are about to do or say something mean to another child, tell them to question that too. It doesn't matter how 'annoying' they judge another person to be, being nasty back never teaches another person a lesson. Give them a short check-list: Is this true? Is this fair? How will others feel about this? 'I might feel justified now but will I regret pressing the send button tomorrow?'

■ **Show them how to spot the warning signs**: Children have more conflicts now partly because the technology they use is so instantaneous that it removes the stages of feeling and reflection that used to precede many fall-outs. Tell them, when they feel the shot of adrenaline that makes them want to post something risky, to give themselves time for it to pass. If they feel the angry, primal side of their brain – which doesn't think about consequences – kicking in, ask them to decide their response only when their more rational, higher thinking has taken back control. Ask them to assess the seriousness of a comment – and go and do something else – to give their fight-or-flight response a chance to die down.

THE BOTTOM LINE: *In all this, there should be one underlying value: that your child should never do or say anything online that they would not say to someone in person.*

Who climbs the highest on the social ladder?

'I felt sorry for a girl in my class because no one liked her. One day, I went and sat with her at lunch. But then none of my friends would sit with me because they thought it would make them look bad. Afterwards the friends in my squad told me, "You should have sat with us, not her".'
Bronwen, 13

'When you meet people, you don't look at who they are. You look at what they wear, where they'd fit in.'
Jackson, 13

As Lisa emptied out the contents of her seven-year-old daughter Anna's school bag one evening, she expected to find the normal collection of crumpled homework sheets and mislaid permissions slips.

Instead the type-written note she discovered turned out to be a directive of a different kind. Written in bullet points, the A4 sheet was titled 'Gang rules'. It laid out a set of instructions from the clique's self-appointed leader, Louise, including a hierarchy of command for its five members.

Lisa, 41, a mother-of-two, said: 'It outlined the laws, one being that the girl who wrote it was 'the leader' and the others couldn't play with anyone else.'

So why do some children take charge like this – and why do others so easily go along with it? The answer is once again to be found in our basic hard-wiring. From the outset, humans are pack animals who stick together for protection. The idea of safety in numbers goes back to when we depended on each other for shelter, support and food gathering.

Indeed, sociologists have found that humans still band together for no other reason than to be part of a group. Numerous experiments have revealed how just putting people in the same shirt or telling them they have the same tastes (even when they don't), can make them clump together and feel hostile against other groups who are even the slightest bit different.

For young people who are looking for an identity, belonging to a group gives them security, but like all things in human relationships, nothing is simple. Once in a group, social scientists have also found that a pecking order soon forms.

In many ways it's understandable. In any group of humans, allocating members different tasks according to their talents, strengths or intelligence makes it stronger and work more efficiently.

Yet at the same time, there is always a battle for the top spot among the more dominant members, because humans have an inbuilt drive for status. According to researchers at the National Institute of Mental Health, scans have found the brain circuitry associated with this desire to be top dog. They found that different brain areas are activated when a person moves up or down the pecking order. When we go up a notch, we get the same hit as we do when we win a cash jackpot on a gambling machine. Adolescent brains have also been found to derive more pleasure from social acceptance than adult brains do.

To add to the mix, young people are also particularly prone to giving each other judgmental labels – and many are not complimentary, like 'geek', 'loser' and 'basic' (meaning ordinary and unexceptional). To make out something is wrong or lacking in others also makes them feel superior or special at a time of their lives when they are most unsure of themselves.

This is also because the human mind finds it easier to sort people into categories. This mental short-hand makes it possible to pigeon-hole others, without taking the time and effort to get to know them as individuals. This really kicks in at secondary school when children are overwhelmed by being with so many people their age. To make sense of their surroundings, the first thing they do is shape-sort their peers to fit social stereotypes.

So with all these dynamics at play – the drive to dominate, form hierarchies and stereotype – it's easy to see how cliques form.

It's around Year Four that these more clearly defined friendship groups start to emerge. The first lines may start to be drawn when a child no longer wants to invite the whole class to a birthday party, and starts to select preferred friends for sleepovers. These cliques become more defined at the start of secondary school. When they arrive, young people are mainly attracted to others who have similar levels of social status, self-esteem and maturity, as well as similar interests and clothes. Boys also tend to form groups based on what sport they like to play, their physical size and sexual maturity plus other interests such as music and video games.

As a group forms, how the clique behaves will start to be directed by the personality of the girl or boy who has the most influence. If it is led by a young person who has naturally risen to the top because they have of a mix of social intelligence and leadership, then they may use their social power for the good, as I will discuss in Part Four.

If, however, the leader has risen to its peak because lax conditions at home have allowed them to feel they can not only manipulate adults, but peers as well – or if they feel out of control of their own lives and are trying to fill that void by controlling or pulling rank over others – the effect on the group as a whole can be negative.

As social capital has increasingly become seen as the only commodity worth having, children in any kind of high status clique may end up with too much influence. At the peak of cliquiness, in the first half of secondary school, members can get conferred with almost mini-celebrity status, amplified by the visible strength of their social media followings.

Yet this growing cliquiness within classrooms is not good for any of our children. Those within the groups feel under pressure to maintain their positions at all costs. Some of those who feel left out live with the feeling that they are somehow not good enough at a formative time of their lives – especially as studies show that both boys' and girls' self-esteem falls off a cliff between the age of about 13 and 15.

But as we shall see in the next part of the book, if parents can help children decode the social pressures swirling around them, they are better able to stay afloat, rather than get sucked under by them.

THE BOTTOM LINE: *Humans will always form themselves into groups and have a tendency to decide who should be on the inside and who should be on the outside. By talking about these pressures, kids can stand up to them better.*

PART TWO
HOW TO UNDERSTAND YOUR CHILD'S SOCIAL LIFE

'My best friend texted me in the summer and said he was going to another school. The last time I saw him was at the house of a friend of both of ours before the new term began. He sat on the bed and started deleting all the contacts from our school on his phone in front of me. He said: "Not gonna lie. I've already deleted you." Then I heard him in the bathroom next door suggesting to my other friend they go downstairs to get away from me. It was the worst afternoon of my life.'
George, 12

'The girl who sits next to my son in class puts her pencil case in between them because she says she doesn't like having to sit next to him. I wish I could be a fly on the wall and work out what's really going on.'
Zainab, 32, mother-of-two

'I blocked my friend on Instagram and Snapchat during a really nasty row and my friend blocked me back. Then she blocked all my friends too, which I thought was taking it a bit far. When my friends asked her why she did it, she said; "You never know what I'm going to post." That sounded like she was threatening to say horrible things about me. She said she wouldn't unblock any of my mates, until I'd unblocked her.'
Bisma, 12

'All the comments on my daughter's pictures are from her close girlfriends, complimenting her. At first, it looks lovely that it's so positive. But flattering each other also seems to be the way girls signal to others that they are in the same friendship group. It's when they don't comment, or post something that could be taken either way, that the tensions start.'
Jane, 50, mother-of-one

Even for a 14-year-old girl mooching around in her pyjamas on a Sunday morning, Ruby is unusually monosyllabic.

After some snappy interchanges with her mum, Hannah, in which Ruby bemoans the lack of food in the (full) fridge and tells her she is 'annoying' her (for smiling in her direction), Ruby finally reveals what's really bothering her when she's asked about her plans for the day.

'Nothing,' she snaps. 'Everyone's at Maya's.'

Ruby does not need to say another word. Immediately, Hannah knows what this means. For weeks, the seven girls in Ruby's friendship group have been talking about a big sleepover at Maya's dad's house. There had been some tensions in the gang, but Ruby had still been included in discussions about what movies they would watch, what they'd eat, and where they'd sleep. But a firm date had never materialised and it hadn't been mentioned for a while. When Ruby had checked her phone the night before, she understood why. She saw the tiny cartoon avatars of her friends congregating at the house on geolocation map app SnapMaps.

These ups and downs are inevitable in human relationships. But when things like this happen, parents can feel very lost about what to do or what to say. For one thing, we find it inconceivable that anyone could be so cruel to our funny, sweet, adorable child. It's also made very confusing by the fact that from the outside, young people's social lives are not easy to understand. When things are going badly – whether it's a temporary blip or they just don't seem to 'fit in', our children may feel too ashamed to tell us they are being rejected. It means that we adults often feel left in the dark and powerless to help.

Have you ever looked at your child's social groups and wondered what's really going on? Why some youngsters seem to hold more sway – yet others seem to be on the sidelines? Have you ever wondered who gets to magically decide who's in and who's out?

Yet, while so much of this seems unfathomable to parents, a growing range of penetrating research is unravelling how children's social lives work. Although you will probably never get chapter and verse on who said what to who, and why, having a field guide can finally give you a sense of direction.

What makes a child popular?

'The popular boys are fit and good at sport. It's not that they are necessarily nasty. They're just not very friendly.'
Simon, 12

'I have just started secondary school and I am not sure what 'popular' means any more. I used to think it meant you are a person that lots of people like because you are a nice person. But at my new school it seems to mean that your parents are rich, and that you are pretty and thin.'
Vanessa, 11

Most of us remember only too well the roles we were assigned at school.

Maybe you were one of 'the swots', 'the sporty ones', 'the emos' or in the 'cool' clique? And whatever group you were in, although it was never spoken about, somehow everyone knew what rung you occupied on the social ladder.

That placement made a difference to what you did at break times, how you dressed, where you sat at lunch and who you spoke to most during the school day.

Long after we've stopped pacing the school corridors, and created independent lives of our own, how popular we were with our peers still stays with us. Even though we suspect that only a few of the most admired people from those formative years ever lived up to their rich promise, many parents still hope for popularity for their children because, at their age, we so desperately craved that admiration ourselves.

As protective parents, we also imagine social status to be like a mystical force-field, which will somehow keep our kids safe from rejection, exclusion and the humiliation of being the last to be picked in PE or finding there's no seat saved for you in the school dining room.

But do we need to be careful what we wish for?

As social scientists have put popularity under the microscope, they have found being this status is not as enviable as it might seem.

They have found that there are two types of popularity. According to the work of Yale psychology Professor Mitch Prinstein, 30 per cent of young people are popular for the right reasons – because they are both visible and likeable.

However, the other 70 per cent have a combination of more evolved social skills, and more dominant personalities, which they use to try and wield power over others. They are feared, rather than liked.

Only the first group consistently turn their popularity into success in adulthood. They are more likely to end up in better relationships, with more fulfilling jobs and even better health. The second group have been found to be more likely to end up anxious and depressed in adulthood, if they are unable to live up to their reputation. Yet at school, the two types often get confused by both children and adults.

Nor is popularity as enviable as it looks because it's like walking in high heels all the time. People may look up to you, but you are always in danger of falling over. Once they have risen to the top of the tribe, children feel they need to work hard to keep impressing others and maintaining their status.

When the young are elevated to the status of mini-celebrities, they feel they have standards of fashion and looks to uphold. They feel they have to invest more on social media to maintain their shiny veneer of success, often compromising their true selves to uphold their image, and losing themselves in the process.

While they may have lots of people wanting to be close to them, a veneer of confidence may really be all they have in common. Once a child is at the centre of the hive, there is also the stress of having so many relationships to maintain and keeping all the acolytes buzzing around you happy.

Furthermore, classmates see the most popular children in secondary schools more as one-dimensional figureheads than real people, making them the target of envy and gossip. A snippet about a popular child has more currency so it will be spread faster. It may also be circulated passive-aggressively by others who'd like to see members of the popular set brought down a peg or two, and want to advance their own place in the social hierarchy.

One admired 13-year-old told me how she was shocked when, after she got in trouble with a teacher for leaving her text book at home, another classmate told her: 'I love seeing you fail.' She was shocked at how the remark revealed the covert hostility lurking among some of her peers who assumed she 'had it all'.

Of course, most children are neither classed as popular or unpopular by their peers. They fall into the middle – and really that is the safest place to be. So if you hope for anything for your child, in their social lives, let it be that they have a band of loyal, good friends around them, who like them for themselves, not for where they fit in.

How classrooms break down into bands

You might assume that the social make-up of a class varies from year to year. But when asked, children will consistently say their classes fall into roughly the same bands of popular and unpopular people.

In a range of studies, social scientists have asked children which peers they like the most and which they like the least.

The children who get the most likes and fewest dislikes are classed as 'popular'. The ones who get the fewest positive and fewest negatives responses were classed as 'neglected'. The ones who get hardly any positive votes – and lots of negative nominations – are classified as 'rejected'.

According to the research, here's how it breaks down:

- **15 per cent: Popular children.** When asked, these are the children their classmates say they'd most like to be friends with. This is because they have qualities or talents like being attractive, stylish or good at sport, which other children admire, as well as more advanced social skills and greater confidence. Boys are more likely to fall into this category at the start of secondary school if they are good at sport and physically more mature or if they are funny. Girls will fall into this band at this stage too if they are socially assertive and seem to effortlessly wear the 'right clothes' and know what to do and say.

- **45 per cent: Accepted children.** Some people want to be close to them, and they have a group of good friends, but they are not as sought after as the popular children. Few people intensely dislike them either. This is the solid core of the class.

- **20 per cent: Controversial children.** Some of their classmates really like them, but some intensely dislike them. This may be because they are very boisterous, hyperactive, unpredictable or disruptive.

- **10 per cent: Neglected children.** These children are ignored by their peers possibly because they are very socially anxious or lacking in confidence. As they don't have friends to protect them, they might be a target for bullying.

- **10 per cent: Rejected children.** These are children who are disliked by a lot of their classmates and have no friends in the class – and few people want to risk being seen with them. Children may fall into this group if they have learning or communication issues which means they are not picking up social cues, or they have missed out on learning social skills at home. They can try to cope by giving in and trying to disappear or by becoming aggressive, and looking for vulnerable children to bully.

Now it's true, at first, this research feels difficult to accept. Why can't our lovely children just be appreciated for who they are? Yet any parent will remember the social hierarchy they were part of when they were at school. It just hurts to hear our children are being ranked in the same way.

So why do these bands form – and how does it help for parents to recognise them?

The answer is that as part of our survival mechanism, the needs of the group always come first. As child psychologist Dr Michael Thompson has explained: 'Any class is a drama that requires different characters. The hierarchy and the roles are "assigned" by the universal forces at work in the group. Many different roles are needed in group life, and the scripts are given to children based on their temperaments and their willingness to play the role.'

If a role is open, say for the teacher's pet or class clown, then the children with the most suitable talents will find themselves stepping into those roles, without realising why. But it's important to take comfort that these findings show that only a small number of children are truly struggling – and with the right targeting, both parents and teachers can help.

Just like in any academic subject, there is always someone who ends up at the bottom of the class. Sadly, it's the same with social pecking orders. Yet that is not a reason to leave them there. If a child were struggling in maths, we'd take steps to make sure that this deficit didn't cause too many long-term problems. We'd give them extra tuition, coaching, take them back to basics and help them spot where they are going wrong. So it is with social skills. Most of the time, parents do not need to get involved in academic subjects. And most of the time, they don't need to get directly involved in their children's social lives either.

However, when a lack of social skills threatens to impact their futures, then, as we will discuss in Part Three, young people need guidance to help them do better.

When we recognise where our children fit, it means the parents and teachers of those bumping along the bottom will know how best to intervene. Most of all, parents need to show these more vulnerable children that this is a hierarchy fostered most intensively within the hothouse of the classroom. They will be able to remind struggling kids that there will always be others who will willingly be their friends in the wider world. Eventually, they will find their tribe.

How friendship grows and changes through childhood

Last year, your nine-year-old son scooted up and down the road with kids from the neighbourhood he didn't know, at the annual summer street party.

This year, he refuses to leave home on the grounds that he doesn't know anyone. When you do coax him out, he will only hover near the adults and complain that he's bored and wants to go home. All this leaves you wondering where your chatty, sociable, little boy has disappeared to.

In the same way as babies learn to crawl before they take their first steps and learn to walk before they can run, children go through clear phases in their social relationships. Understanding these shifts can help parents work out when it's perfectly normal and when a child might need a helping hand.

Nought to two

From the moment they are born, babies are looking for friends. The first one is their primary carer after birth, most usually their mother.

Even at this early age, by talking, playing and responding to their cues parents and carers teach them about the to and fro of social communication. As their first companions, parents' love and attention is already setting them up for good relationships outside of the family too. Children who are confident in their relationship with you have been found to get on better with their peers as they grow up, because they have better communication skills and are more trusting and open to others.

From around the age of around six months, children start to look further afield in the wider world for friends. When they see another child their age, they will try and move towards them to find out more. However, the fact they will often swat the new companion or grab their hair demonstrates they view them more as interesting new toys than other people.

Yet gradually they learn that others have feelings too. When they see another child being distressed, toddlers as young as 14 months will have the urge to help – by offering a toy as a comfort – because they know that's what would make them feel better.

However, at this age, they don't understand each other's thought processes enough to play directly together, so instead they play side by side. Really they are keeping an eye on what the other child is doing, and often copying, as if to say: 'Me too.'

Three to five

Until this age a friend is whomever you happen to be playing with at the time. But by three, children will start to seek out the company of playmates they particularly like.

When social scientists looked at what made children friends, it was found that they were most drawn to peers with the same level of play, social skills and assertiveness.

By this age, youngsters are also becoming aware of the differences between them – and will often, but not always, prefer to play more with children of the same sex.

Your child and their playmates are now starting to give each other roles in their games of make-believe, using imaginary or real objects. Pretend play allows children to learn skills they can transfer to the real world, like problem solving, making themselves understood, taking turns and learning the art of compromise.

According to anthropologist Desmond Morris, social conflicts at this age break out for three reasons: a child takes a toy without permission, says they don't like what the other one is doing and asserts they can do it better, or calls them names.

Studies have found children who can communicate clearly at this age play better and for longer with others. That's because words will help them cooperate and share better, rather than using non-verbal tactics like snatching, whining or screaming.

Already peer pressure is starting to take hold. Researchers have found that when asked to make a decision, children this age will already go with the majority, whether they know it to be right or wrong.

Five to eight

Children are starting to learn that other people have different thoughts and feelings from them, a process called 'theory of mind'. This means that they are becoming more sensitive to how they are judged by others. Friends are also becoming increasingly important to make themselves accepted and validated.

As children try to work out who they are, and seek reassurance that they are making the right choices in what they like and how they look, they generally seek out the friends who they think are most similar to them.

Girls, who according to the research tend to be hard-wired to enjoy language and value connection more than boys, are now tending to form smaller friendship groups. They may be seeking out a best friend, too, to mirror back their own interests and make them feel 'special'. And while girls will set up dates to meet each other at break times to try their favourite role-play games, boys tend to join the nearest game with whoever is around. While boys tend to be more interested in physical activities outside themselves, girls tend to be more interested in each other.

Children are also starting to identify themselves with certain traits, like being good at football, ballet or drawing – and may now be seeking to impress each other by showing off their skills.

Nine to eleven

In this phase, children's friendships are getting closer and more meaningful, but also more complicated. More and more, they are becoming sensitive to the growing differences between them and watching each other to see who's showing the first signs of puberty.

Within friendship groups, there will now be unwritten rules about how members act, behave and dress. For girls, this can include minutiae as minor as the right height to wear their ponytails, and what length school socks to wear. For some boys, the judgement may centre on haircuts, shoes and physical skills.

As they are becoming more status orientated, children may ask for only certain brands of clothes, school bags or even pencil cases to show they fit in.

By the end of this phase, youngsters are also developing more complicated expectations of what it means to be a good friend – and testing out values like trust, reliability and loyalty. They will view their best friends chiefly as fellow musketeers who should stick up for each other through thick and thin. As children build a sense of their private self, separate from their parents, secrets are becoming more important now. It means they will feel especially let down if a friend betrays a confidence.

Twelve to fifteen

Starting secondary school is just as much of an upheaval for your child as starting nursery was. Because children are so uncertain about themselves, the ones who rise to the top of the social ladder will initially be those who act older or look more mature.

Be prepared for attempts at status-building at the start of secondary school, followed by friendship break-ups when the mates they first got together with aren't such a natural fit after all.

Some children may also start hanging around the edges of popular groups because they want to borrow status from them – but these children are often most at risk because they are seen as 'wannabes' and can be whispered about or made fun of for trying too hard.

As young people enter this crucial period, they may start to define themselves not just by who they are friends with, but also who they don't want to be friends with.

There is also a period of adjustment for parents for another reason: they notice their children are now more interested in what their peers think, rather than anything their parents have to say. Indeed, there is a biological reason. Scans have found that the reward centres in adolescent brains are triggered by interactions with people of their own age far more easily than adult brains. To a young person, it means that staying in contact with and meeting up with their 'squad' will now feel like a matter of life and death. To maintain these relationships and proclaim them publicly, young teens will also spend a lot of time strengthening their peer bonds by taking videos and selfies and liking each other's posts on social media for all to see.

Not surprisingly, this is the age when parents often hit peak exasperation due the amount of time children want to spend on their phones. But it's worth remembering that it's not so much their gadgets they are addicted to. They are actually addicted to knowing what their friends are up to – and terrified of missing out on anything.

Emotions can also run high now, as young people make their first awkward attempts to connect romantically with each other. There will be jockeying and competition now to see who gets a boyfriend or girlfriend first, which will confer status. Often tiffs will blow up because there may be competition for the same people. There may well also be rows between girls over gossip and the issue of 'reputation' – who's acting like 'a slag' and who's not. Boys may also come into conflict over liking the same girl.

All too often these issues can spill out into conflict on social media, because emotional teens haven't yet developed the self-restraint to control their impulses.

The pre-frontal cortex of the brain is critical in making decisions and helping to understand cause and effect. But because this area is still very much in development for them, young people find it hard to stop themselves reacting. Combine this with their freedom to say and post virtually what they like on social media, and you can see how rows quickly escalate.

Fifteen to eighteen

At last, you may well feel the stormy waters of your child's friendships are starting to calm a little now. As young people have developed a stronger sense of their own identity, peer pressure no longer has as much sway.

By now, the good news is the power of the 'mean girl' or clique leader has also hit its peak. Youngsters who have used relational aggression may now find their power is starting to diminish as their peers get wise to their tactics and start to distance themselves. So as a parent, it may seem as though there are not quite as many dramas, put-downs or upsets as there were at the start of secondary school.

Until now, male and female friendship groups have mainly stayed in separate boy/girl groups. But by this age, the genders start to mix more socially – and relax around each other – so young people can experiment with getting to know each other in a safe context.

Gradually some members of the friendship groups will start to pair off. As their new partners' needs start to come first, old friendship groups become looser. Those who have stayed loyal are still valued, leaving young people with a closer band of more trusted friends.

The hold of the clique

'Clique is a girl's word. I have a group of close friends, but I call them a gang.'
Adam, 11

'When there was a fall-out with one of the cliques at my school, the bossiest girl reposted some of the pictures they'd taken together as a group at parties on social media... this time with a girl's whole body scribbled out. It was her way of saying: "You're not in our group any more." Brutal.'

Leah, 13

'There's a netball clique, my clique, who are the "cool girls", the TLC clique, named because the girls in it have names starting with those letters. But I'd say people only think cliques are bad if they can't get into them. I think they are just jealous. But it's true that if you are in a clique, you do have to put up with hanging around with people you don't like – because it would lead to too much beef if you said something. It means I sometimes have to pretend I like people when I don't.'

Yasmine, 14

'My son in Year 7 says he feels excluded as there's a clique of boys in his class who went to the same primary who are good at cricket. Though he seems to be on good terms with them individually, if he is hanging round near them, they ignore him when he speaks.'

Marcella, 39, mother-of-two

Cliques tend to get a bad name perhaps due to their portrayal in films like *Mean Girls*. They also have a reputation for promoting negative peer pressure, and for hurting others by making them feel less important than they are. But while they do get a bad name, it's only natural for young people to seek the safety and security of a steady friendship group.

Yet even when they have found their group, there is often anxiety lurking. As we've discussed, the insiders worry about maintaining their position, and may sacrifice some of their independence in order to stay inside the walls of their circle. At times, they may act in ways contrary to their better judgement, by going along with peer pressure or by presenting a snobby or superior tone to outsiders, in order to maintain their prestige or exclusivity.

As educator Rosalind Wiseman, author of *Queen Bees and Wannabes*, has pointed out, each member has their own role in the hierarchy that naturally forms. The best way to help your son or daughter understand how they may be influenced by being in a clique is to help them work out their position within it.

If they are on the inside, helping your child to understand the powerful peer group forces at work will help them to hold on to their individuality. If they are on the outside, understanding those group dynamics will help youngsters decide whether they really want to be a part of a clique at all. Often the happiest children are those who float between friendship groups, not feeling the need to pledge allegiance to any of them. Beyond that, if children understand the same politics are played out again and again in social groups, they will stop blaming themselves when things go wrong. By understanding the dynamics, they are more likely to be able a keep a clear head and step away from the drama.

HOW TO HELP

- **It's quality over quantity**: Children don't need a lot of friends to be happy. So assure your child there's no requirement to be in the 'in-crowd'. Two or three good friends with whom they can share confidences is enough to enjoy school.

- **Get them to ask questions**: Ask your child to think about why they like someone. Is it because they like being around someone or because they think it looks good to be in their camp? Does this friendship make your child feel good – or insecure and uncertain? It should feel easy, not like a power struggle. Remind them that friends are not rungs on a ladder to help them gain popularity. Help them notice when they are not being themselves, just to fit in, so that they understand the pressures acting on them.

- **Help them to work out their role**: Ask them to draw a friendship tree, like a mind map, to lay out all their social relationships. By putting them down on paper, they will better understand how they fit into the machinery.

- **Give support**: If your child is one of the children who does seem in demand, help him or her pick and choose the events he or she goes to and manage their time. Explain the difference between good popularity, which is based on people liking him or her for who he or she is, and bad popularity, which is when others are afraid to cross them because of their social power. Ask him or her to use their social status for the good and stand up for others.

- **Know the difference between a friendship group and a clique**: Children don't like the word clique because they know it has negative connotations – so they'll often come up with other names like 'gang' or 'squad'. The truth is it's only a clique if the members define themselves more by who they don't like, rather than who they do – and they actively police its walls, forcing members to stay locked in and keeping would-be incomers out. It's also a negative clique if there's overbearing pressure for everyone to be alike, if the group thinks they are better than anyone else and members are laughed at, excluded or punished if they step out of line.

- **Give affirmation at home**: Affirm your child's views at home so they are not so needy for approval elsewhere. Help your child develop other talents and qualities so they don't feel dependent on their popularity rating at school. Give unconditional love at home so they know they always have a secure base.

- **Help your child move on**: If other children in the group they aspire to join are not inviting your child to parties or sleepovers, it's time for them to start developing other friendships. Otherwise at a formative time in their lives, their self-worth will suffer. Help them see how much they would have to compromise themselves to fit in. Suggest they ask themselves questions like: 'Is this the right group for me?', 'Do I have to dress or act differently to fit in?', 'Do I feel comfortable here?' Help your child to recognise the group dynamics and that there's no point trying to belong if they're not a good fit.

- **Remember it's a phase**: As children get older and start to get a feel for who they are, they outgrow the need to be part of controlled clique. Cliques peak in the early years of secondary school when children are at their most insecure. Most start to dissolve by Years 11 and 12 as young people become more secure within their own identities.

- **Explain that it's possible to be a free agent:** Not every young person needs the refuge of a clique. Tell your child there is another way. Those who are free agents, who step away from drama and who have friends in a variety of different groups, often end up being the most respected by their peers.

Who's who in the girls' cliques?

According to the research of US educator Rosalind Wiseman, popular cliques break down into these roles.

The Queen Bee: A combination of charm, confidence and social sophistication will take this girl to the head of the group. She is widely admired for being pretty and stylish. The fact that she might have been able to convince adults how mature she is may also mean she is used to being able to control others and get her way. To teachers, she is often skilled enough to give a 'butter wouldn't melt' appearance. As a result, she may get to be Form Captain in the classroom and land the bigger roles in the school plays, reinforcing her social power. This will also add to her belief that she is above the law. No one in the class wants to get on the wrong side of the Queen Bee. This is because if she is willing to use her social power negatively and she decides to exclude another child, others will back her because they are terrified of getting on her wrong side. Yet it can also be tough in the Queen Bee position because it takes a lot of mental energy for this girl to stay on top of her game. If you are the Queen Bee's parent, while you may be pleased she seems very popular and in demand, you may be worried by how preoccupied your child is with arranging her social life (parents are purposely no longer involved). She will feel the pressure to stay ahead of the pack in the style stakes, in order to present a flawless image, so she remains admired by her followers. You may also find she spends a disproportionate amount of time on social media managing her image and friendships.

The Sidekick: The Sidekick looks like the Queen Bee's best friend, but she is also the second in command and does her bidding. Her job is to present a united front with the Queen Bee. If you are the sidekick's parent, you may be worried your daughter puts the Queen Bee on too much of a pedestal and allows her to boss her around.

The Banker: The Banker looks nice enough but her skill is being good at listening to other girls and banking information when they confide their secrets in her. Then, at strategic moments, she will dispense nuggets to other group members, triggering upsets and tears. However, the Banker will still emerge unscathed. Other clique members won't retaliate, as they are frightened to cross her because of how much she knows about them too.

The Messenger: When rows break out, it's the Messenger who tries to help everyone patch things up. This gives her a key role within the group and makes her feel valued, but part of her enjoys the drama. However, her position is not strong, so she is quickly dropped or made fun of if other members get tired of her.

The Pleaser/Wannabe: This girl is desperate to get into the group, and will do anything to prove she deserves a place. Despite buying the same clothes and borrowing the same look, it does not come naturally to her – so the others look down on her for trying too hard. She may have low self-esteem already so she is liable to get used. She is one of the most vulnerable members of the group, and parents may need to use some of the techniques described elsewhere in the book to keep her self-worth strong and help her recognise that it's just not worth it. She is easily manipulated so she will do the dirty work of the Queen Bee, like spreading rumours. However, the Wannabe may also be the most dangerous member of the group, because she is the most desperate. To get access to the popular girls, she may have to use gossip to win favour and attention from them, and use excluding behaviour to keep out rivals.

The Torn Bystander: She is one of the quieter and more passive members of the group. To stay inside its walls, she dare not take a stand even if she sees the Queen Bee behaving in ways she doesn't like. She will often get caught in the middle of a row and is torn because she wants to remain part of the group, but doesn't like the way the others act.

The Target: If a member of the group gets above her station or doesn't conform to the rules of her group on dress or behaviour, she becomes the butt of teasing to bring her down a peg. She won't tell anyone because she is so ashamed that she is now being humiliated. She will learn the hard way that it's better to be independent of a group.

The Floater: This is a girl who doesn't care what the other girls think and doesn't feel the need to be in a clique. She chooses friends from a variety of groups, based on whether she likes them or not. She has social power because her peers like who she is as a person – but she does not have as much influence as the Queen Bee. At times, being a Floater can be a lonely position to be in, but by the time she is in year 10 or 11, she will have kept her individuality and won the respect of her peers.

Who's who in the boys' cliques?

While we hear a lot about mean and bitchy behaviour among girls, we tend to assume boys' social lives are much simpler by comparison. How often have you heard that when boys fall out, 'they thump each other and move on'?

In reality, the social life of boys can be just as complex. Although they would never call their friendship groups cliques, boys can also exert power over each other within their close peer groups.

The difference is that there's less jockeying for power, as the roles tend to be more fixed – and boys talk less about the fall-out because they feel it's a sign of weakness. In their world, the pecking order tends to be more clearly established along the lines of which boys conform best to stereotypically masculine behaviour or who excels most at sought-after skills, like sports, who is the funniest or who shows the most leadership skills.

Indeed, researchers studying pre-schoolers found that boys tend to try and establish their dominance as soon as they meet a new boy, from an early age, for example snatching a toy to see how the other reacts. When some learn they often come out on top – and others don't resist, a hierarchy begins to form. Dominant children, however, only keep their places as leaders if they have the social savvy to inspire admiration and maintain their relationships. Once established, the alpha boy stays in place and is not challenged unless there is a serious chink in his armour.

Here being strong, in control, aggressive, tough, athletic and assertive are what will take you to the top. Boys will often lose out if they're un-sporty, sensitive, 'soft', try too hard or if they show their feelings.

Yet considering that girls are deemed to be so socially attuned, it's boys who better understand the social dynamics they are caught up in. This is probably because their social power is so clearly based on a more obvious combination of physical size and/or confidence. They know that other boys don't necessarily like the ones in the popular group. As educator Rosalind Wiseman points out in her book *Ringleaders and Sidekicks*, they know that it's not worth their while getting on the wrong side of the popular boys because they would lose in a fight. In the same way that girls have a ranking of the prettiest, boys tend to know exactly who is capable of beating up whom.

Boys' cliques also exercise power in different ways. While girls' cliques use the threat of exclusion to keep control over the ranks, boys enforce their rules by making members feel feeble if they don't stick to the unwritten rules.

According to Wiseman, here's how their roles break down:

The Ringleader: Like the Queen Bee, this is the boy who the others want to be. The Ringleader isn't necessarily the loudest in the group, but he has alpha male-type charisma, physical presence and is savvy enough to know other people's weak points. Whether it's clothes – especially trainers – or music, it's up to him to decide what's cool, funny or stupid and how the group will spend their time.

The Associate: Like the Sidekick, he works in tandem with his best friend, the Ringleader, to keep them at the head of the pack. He is chattier, better liked and probably socially more astute than the leader, but is happy being second-in-command because it's less pressure.

The Bouncer: Well-built and intimidating, the Bouncer performs the same function as he does in a club. He takes up a lot of space, is not well-liked – but he is feared. He does what he is told by the pack leaders, but doesn't have the verbal or emotional skills to break out on his own. The Bouncer makes his group more visible and helps them 'own' various spots around the school and school grounds, so they can be seen as the alpha males.

The Entertainer: This boy is the joker in the pack and his job is to make fun of himself to defuse tension, even if it's at his own expense. When he talks, everyone's always waiting for the punch-line but it means he has to keep up the act and never gets taken seriously.

The Conscience: He is seen as the 'nice boy' of the group – and reminds the other members of the rules and how not to get into trouble. He may be made fun of for being a goody-two-shoes. The boys keep him around anyway to help them get out of a tight spot, or if they get caught doing things like drinking, smoking, treating girls badly or taking other risks.

The Fly: This is the hanger-on who tries to gain access to the group by showing off or bragging. At first the other boys might use him but will eventually find him so annoying that he could end up being rejected.

The Champion: Like the Floater, the Champion is the boy who's strong and charismatic enough to tick all the popularity boxes. However he likes people for who they are and doesn't insist people change their ways to be friends with him. Like the Floater, he can feel distant from his peers at the start of secondary school but ultimately staying a free agent will be worth it.

How boys' and girls' friendships are different

> 'In my experience as a parent of boys and girls, boys like to play in herds – they run around together, play football and action games. Not all of them are like this of course. But they aren't really interested in who they are playing with, just that they can have fun in the moment.'
> **Danielle, 48, mother-of-three**

> 'You have to look like you don't care, even if your friend has treated you like cr*p. You don't want other people to say you're making a big deal.'
> **Joe, 13**

Watch a group of four- and five-year-olds for ten minutes in the playground, and it doesn't take long to spot that most boys and girls will lean naturally towards different styles of play. The girls may start teaming up in pairs to have a go on the see-saw. This delicate balancing act will continue when they move to role-play games like shops, vets or doctors. Meanwhile many of the boys will have seized on whatever object they can find and turned it into a sword or a gun. They are likely to be running around in groups, bellowing war cries like: 'You're the enemy' and 'I killed you!'

Of course, these are broad – and increasingly unfashionable – generalisations. Some girls want to kick balls and jump in leaf piles too, while other boys are generally happier with less boisterous activities, like reading or making things. No doubt as we move into a more gender fluid age, and sexual stereotyping begins to dilute, some of these differences will start to dissolve because some are due to the way young children are socialised. However, a body of research has also found there seems to be some biological basis for the different ways boys and girls interact.

A range of research has found that boys generally play in more physically active ways – and even the more energetic girls don't have the same physical drive to run around. One explanation is that MRI scans of children's brains have found that boys explore the world by feeling, hearing and seeing, and girls by talking and thinking about it. (Yet even when boys get rough, they seem to know intuitively where to draw the line – and it doesn't mean that they will grow up to be violent.)

While some of it may be conditioning, some of these differences in play preferences seem to be partly down to the influence of androgens – or male hormones – on baby boys' brains, while they are still in the womb. Although these will vary by individual, generally girls' brains get more oestrogen in utero and this builds the hard-wiring that makes them more verbal. They start speaking earlier, and they use and construct longer, more complex sentences, which makes fantasy play so entertaining for them. They also produce more of the bonding hormone oxytocin, which makes them value social bonds more.

How girls conduct their relationships seems to be different too. They have been found to remember emotional events more clearly, which means they play and re-play the drama of an argument over and over. They are more likely to try and analyse what went wrong, and also seek new female bonds to help make themselves feel better and re-build their networks.

Furthermore, research has found they fall out over different things – girls are more likely to row over behaviour than boys, while boys are more likely to clash over possession of objects. Because boys are more likely to use their size and physical strength to intimidate, they are also more likely to bully physically than girls, while girls intimidate verbally.

Indeed, how children use words to build relationships also differs. Psychologist Deborah Tannen, professor of sociolinguistics at America's Georgetown University, points out that while girls use words to build rapport, boys use them to build status.

All this could account for the widely held belief that while boys bash their way through school – and then forget any conflicts the next day – girls are more complicated socially. However, as we shall hear, increasingly it's being recognised that boys just work harder to project a 'couldn't care less' attitude.

Yet in all this talk of the gender divide, it's also important to remember that boys' and girls' friendships are still more similar than they are different. What they have in common is that both genders want a deep sense of connection, however they express it.

How to tackle boys' friendship problems

'My 15-year-old son says that when boys say horrible things to each other they present it as a joke – but actually they really mean it.'
Helen, 43

> 'When my eldest son, who is 14, became the punch bag for other boys to pick on to show how tough they were, my husband told him he had to "man up".'
>
> **Noor, 44**

For many stereotypically male boys, it's essential that their superhero masks are never seen to slip. Those on the receiving end of meanness are meant to deal with even the most vicious insults, on the grounds that it's 'all a joke'.

Yet even if they don't show it, it's a mistake to think that boys don't suffer as much with friendship issues. They are simply keener to make it look like friendship problems don't bother them as much. They are more likely than girls to think they should suffer in silence, brush it off, or laugh about it.

So why do boys feel this way?

In part, it's to do with how they are brought up. Hard though it may be to acknowledge, without realising it parents often unknowingly perpetuate the belief that boys should hide their hurts and be able to look after themselves as soon as possible.

From an early age, the outdated perception exists that straight-acting boys should learn to 'take it like a man' – like the comic book heroes and superhero dolls they are often given to play with.

If a boy hurts himself on the sports pitch, social scientists have observed that boys are consistently praised more readily for hiding that they are in pain and for picking themselves up as soon as possible. In other words, they must be able to break free from the comfort of their parents as soon as possible, and raised to be the opposite of girls, who are encouraged to stay close and tell us everything.

Of course, it's all done with the best intentions. Even in these days of greater sexual equality, underneath it all many of us still hang on to the belief that boys must grow up, most of all, to be tough, strong and inscrutable men. As we raise them, we unconsciously worry that by letting our sons stay too close, their peers will pick on them for being 'too soft'. Mothers, in particular, may believe they need to step away sooner from their sons than their daughters, emotionally.

But when boys are raised with a code that tells them they have to reject feminine qualities, like being affectionate or emotionally expressive, they end up closing down.

The gender stereotyping that creates this divide starts early. Studies have found mothers are more likely to use emotional words when talking to their four-year-old daughters, compared to their four-year-old sons. It means that boys simply never learn the language of talking about how they feel.

Instead they go the other way, feeling the need to show a macho facade of invulnerability. In turn, this can make them more aggressive with their peers, which only causes more conflict.

Dr William Pollack, assistant clinical professor of psychology at Harvard Medical School, and author of *Real Boys,* believes that for boys to be happy and healthy, they must be allowed to express their feelings just as freely as girls. Instead of believing their femininity will somehow contaminate their sons, mothers should also try to stay close, and boys should be encouraged to have friends of the opposite sex throughout their lives.

In the meantime, just because your son is not coming to you and pouring his heart out, as his sister might, doesn't mean he's not having friendship issues. He may just be keeping his hurt out of sight.

Boys are scarily skilful at putting up a wall to keep others out, and throwing you off a scent when there's a problem. It takes a sensitive parent to circumvent the eye-rolling, diversion tactics and sarcasm boys use to avoid telling you what's bothering them.

- **Look for signs he wants to talk**: If your son keeps hanging around you, offers to help around the house out of the blue or keeps mentioning an issue in passing, however casually, find ways to draw him out using some of the ideas suggested below. When boys are worried and anxious, it can be more difficult for them to articulate exactly what's happening to them so they need help starting the conversation. Other signs may be more fights at home with siblings, a shorter fuse, or more time in his bedroom with the door shut.

- **Help him find the words:** Studies show that children are better at expressing emotions when they have been shown how to describe them by adults. From early childhood, name your own feelings and help him identify his own.

- **Reconnect:** Ask open questions like, 'What's happening in your life?' Don't let your son keep putting you off. If he still feels distant, take him away for some one-on-one time of his choosing so he can relax on his own terms, rather than yours.

- **Use other ways to get him talking:** If you tackle the subject head-on, boys may get self-conscious and close down. If you are curious about his friendships or think there may be a problem, approach it from another angle. When you watch TV or a film with your son, ask him his views on how realistic he thinks it is. Try age appropriate films which touch on boys' friendships, whether it's *Stand*

By Me or *Dead Poets Society*, to get him talking about his own situations with his friends.

- **Talk about gender stereotypes:** Boys can be unkind to each other because they may fear that any emotional dependence on another makes them 'girly'. They are responding to cultural pressure to be stoic and self-sufficient. Bring your son up knowing that there's nothing wrong with having a close connection with someone of their own gender. Make it clear there's a difference between having a gay sexual orientation and enjoying the companionship of a good friend. If you hear him use homophobic language, ask him why he's using these words and what he thinks they mean.

- **Ask other males to guide him:** Because our sons look to male role models to find out what it is to be a man, their fathers, uncles and godfathers can help set more enlightened expectations. Studies have found that boys follow same-sex role models the most.

And if a friendship has gone wrong...

- **Listen without judgement:** When your son does open up, thank him and then listen calmly and without judgement, no matter how angry you feel, to what he describes is happening in his friendship group. If he cries, allow him to do so without comment. Otherwise he could become self-conscious and reminded of his fears that boys are not supposed to show their emotions.

- **Don't dismiss his worries by telling him to ignore them:** This will edge him back towards his boy cave. Beware of coming out with advice to try and 'fix' the situation. As you are not him or his age, you won't fully understand all the complexities of the situation, and he may then close down, because you will have proved to him you haven't got a clue. Instead listen more than you speak, avoid taking sides, help him name how he feels and tell him you are sorry he's going through this and remind him that it will pass.

- **Ask other males to share their experiences:** When there are fractures in a friendship, boys are more likely to distance themselves from their peers because they are not sure what else to do. This is where dads and other male role models in particular, can help by talking about incidents in which they had a fall-out with a male friend, and how they repaired it.

Decide on your values

It's easy, and it feels good, to tell your children to be 'nice' to other people. Rolling this out makes us feel like a responsible parent – in the moment. But this sort of floating statement is too vague for a child to understand how this would work in the real world. Ultimately, our children learn far more from what we do, rather than from what we say. It's in the unavoidable moments of conflict with others that our values get tested the most. If our own behaviour doesn't underpin the words, 'Be kind', those words don't count for much. For example, when a friendship issue flares up in your own relationships, do you blame everyone but yourself? Have you ever been tempted to make fun of others or gossip about others who have crossed you? Do you join with others bitching about 'easy targets' in your social circle? If a friend is giving a mutual acquaintance the silent treatment, do you also cool your relationship with that person rather than be your own person? If we say the words 'Be kind', and then contradict them by not acting kindly ourselves, we invalidate their power altogether. When children have these tests – for example, if they see a classmate being bullied and are tempted to join in – they need values to pull them back to trying to be the best person they can be. Yet in an increasingly 'me-first' society, most of us are too busy responding to the frantic pace of our lives to sit down and decide what values we want to uphold in our families. Yet how can we expect our children to take the higher road if we never tell them what that is?

Stephen Covey, the American speaker and author, recommended parents and children come up with a 'family mission statement' to create a vision of what you are about. 'Good families – even great families – are off-track 90 per cent of the time,' he said. 'What makes them good is they have a clear destination in mind, and they have a flight plan to get there. As a result, when they face the inevitable turbulence and human error, they keep coming back to their plan.'

Every child will find themselves in a difficult situation at some time. They will be encouraged by their friends to ignore other children, or cut them out of a game, or be tempted to join in when others are bitching about people they don't like. Values will help your child better work out what to do in these dilemmas and give them the backbone to take a stand against meanness, whether it's happening to them or to other people.

- **Put them in the real world:** Make values real by talking through dilemmas. Look at the news, whether it's a story about cyberbullying or a heroic act, and talk together about the choices that were involved – and what you and your child would have done in the same situation.

- **Set a good example:** Do you stand up for others in your adult life – or do you stand by and watch? In your own family, if you hear your children being mean about others in the back of the car as you ferry them to a party, do you intervene or do you by-stand and let it pass? There is a difference between allowing children to express legitimate feelings, and silently permitting them to indulge in deliberate bitchiness. If you hear it, ask them their reasons for saying this. Otherwise you are by-standing and tacitly allowing it to continue.

- **Watch your own impulses:** Have you ever felt that little spark of power when you say something unkind about someone else, because it makes you feel superior? Do you express judgemental views about others when you don't know their full situation? If so, watch for that feeling as a warning sign. Ask yourself: 'Do I really need to say this?' Listen to the messages you are sending out as your child is always watching and learning from you.

- **Explain that being kind is better for health and well-being:** According to Dr. Pier Forni, director of The

Civility Initiative at John Hopkins University, teaching your child to be kind also brings long term health benefits. 'Science tells us that when we engage in acts of civility and kindness, both the person on the giving end and the one on the receiving end benefit; it's known as "helper's high". Indeed, a range of studies have found that kinder people tend to live longer and lead healthier lives. By deliberately setting out to teach kindness, remember that you will also be giving your child life-long health benefits.

- **Allow them to defer to you:** Peer pressure is difficult for anyone to resist, let alone children. While your son or daughter is still developing their own road map, it can be hard for them to stick to good values in the heat of the moment. So allow them to borrow yours if they find themselves in compromising positions as they get older. As they spend more time away from home on sleepovers or at parties – where drink or drugs may be on offer – give teens a code word to use so they can call you at any time, and secretly let you know they are in a situation they are not comfortable with, so you can come and collect them.

- **Model conflict resolution:** Many parents shrink from rows and confrontations with others because they don't like the drama. Yet your home can be a safe training ground. Research has found that parents who look at the issue from their children's perspective, are more likely to raise young people who will consider every opinion in an argument and reach resolutions quicker.

- **Let siblings work it out:** Although they can feel like a headache, with the right approach, arguments between siblings who are fairly evenly matched can be a safe practice ground to teach kids how to resolve conflicts, to debate and respect different opinions in a safe space. Praise every step they make towards sorting out their differences.

- **Pick your words:** It can take many years for children to understand the subtleties of sarcasm, so if they are at the receiving end of it from adults and siblings in their family, they can be left feeling confused and hurt. They may also internalise negative messages about themselves like: 'I must be annoying'. It also does not translate well outside the home. When children parrot it in the outside world, it can sound mean and unpleasant. Adding 'Only joking' never makes it OK either.

THE BOTTOM LINE: *Tell your child they may not like everyone, but they can still treat everyone as if they are worthy of dignity and courtesy. Even if another classmate isn't their friend, they can still be polite. Indeed, at the core of every social interaction should be the question: 'Am I treating this person in a way in which I would like to be treated?'*

Training children to tell the difference between a good and a bad friend

Starting from a young age, it's important for your child to learn what a good friend is. This is not only so they can be one themselves, but also so they can identify healthy relationships, both now and for future romantic ones.

A bad friend is someone who:

- Doesn't want you to play with other friends

- Tells you that what you like is stupid

- Laughs at you

- Makes you feel sad

- Pushes you to do things you don't want to do

- Acts as if they are better than you

- Hurts you

- Says they will do something unkind to you if you don't do what they want

- Tells people your secrets

- Tells you that other friends don't like you.

A good friend is someone who:

- Plays with all your friends

- Tells you that you are good at doing stuff

- Doesn't mind if you don't want to do the same things

- You have fun with

- You don't have to play with all the time

- Doesn't require you to like all the same things they do

- Doesn't try and make you do anything as a condition of staying their friend.

How to teach good friendship skills

'I am not talking to you because you're giving me a headache,' rants five-year-old Beatrice into the plastic mobile phone she's just picked out the nursery toy basket. 'I SAID, you're giving me a HEAD-ACHE,' she continues – and everything from the tart tone, to the exasperated expression makes it pretty clear where she's heard it from – the adults in her life.

In Year 7 at secondary school, 11-year-old Hannah is also at a loss as to why, after they were getting on really well yesterday, her best friend Stella has just turned her back on her during break when she asked her if she wanted to go to their usual playground bench.

Indeed, the youngsters most likely to use the silent treatment on their friends are the ones who have experienced it at the hands of their parents. And of course why wouldn't they? A child who has experienced the bewilderment of having a trusted adult go cold on them knows first-hand how devastating it feels and how easy it is to do to others.

Before children make their own social connections, parents are their first friends. A range of studies has found that youngsters who have healthy relationships with the adults in their lives are more likely to have good friendships. When family relationships are warm and secure, it sets up the expectation that their friendships with others will also be safe. When parents respond to their needs, they learn to trust others around them.

As children grow, we continue to influence their friendships with our parenting style. There are four main types – neglectful, permissive, authoritarian and authoritative.

Neglectful parents let children raise themselves on their own, often forgetting to care for their emotional needs, and not knowing much about what's happening at school or in their child's life.

Permissive parents are loving, and attentive, and set out to be their children's best friend, offering plenty of freedom but setting few rules or consequences.

In authoritarian parenting, parents are strict in the 'because I said so' mould, setting out plenty of rules and routine. Here adults don't need to explain themselves or their actions. They are in charge.

It is the authoritative parenting style which has been found to produce the most socially successful children. Authoritative parents set limits but they also relate to their children warmly. They try to shape their behaviour, not just by laying down rules, but also explaining the reasons behind them. They talk rationally about emotional conflicts, rather than using heavy-handed discipline.

To be that parent, it will help if you do the following:

- Listen to your child, rather than lecture

- Take your child's views and feelings into account

- Help them see mistakes as opportunities to learn

- Set up clear consistent rules and explain why these are in place

- Let your child make small choices and show them how to take responsibility for their decisions

- Be honest about your own emotions, talk about your feelings, and give your children the words and opportunities to express their own.

Why do some children make friends more easily than others?

As parents, it's fascinating to watch our children's characters develop. So what forms your child's social personality – and why do some youngsters find it initially easier to make and keep friends than others?

For decades, the nature versus nurture debate has raged – and it applies just as much to our children's social lives. Are some children naturally sociable and outgoing – or do they inherit these traits from us? If we are hesitant around new people, do our children learn to be hesitant too? In this part, I will look at some of the latest research on what might affect friendship development.

One factor is birth order. For example, according to researcher Lisette Schuitemaker, co-author of *The Eldest Daughter Effect*, eldest girls can be the least easy going when it comes to friendships.

This is because when brothers and sisters arrive on the scene, the eldest daughter tends to feel she becomes an equal to her mother, because she is helping her care for the younger children. She can become a 'mini-adult'. This early conditioning may mean oldest sisters are not only more likely to feel a deeper sense of responsibility throughout their lives, but socially may also come across as more intense, serious and perfectionist. They may also be slower to warm up when meeting new people.

Meanwhile middle children have been found to be the more trusting and cooperative in friendships because they've learnt to fit in. They may also handle relationship issues better because they are better at seeing things from both sides. Last-born children have also been found to be sociable and outgoing, but more socially manipulative.

Another factor may be a child's underlying genetic make-up. Any parent who has had more than one child will have noticed basic differences in personality from birth. The beginnings can be traced back to the womb because some of our character is determined by DNA. Researcher Jerome Kagan, found that even in utero, the hearts of the shyer children beat consistently faster than other babies. He concluded that around 10 to 20 per cent come into the world with more aroused nervous systems which make them more jumpy and distressed in response to new situations. These are the babies who are not as quick to smile with new people, and who, as toddlers, are more hesitant with people they do not know. On further inspection it was found that the amygdala, the brain's antennae for threat, is aroused more easily in such children, and triggers more anxious responses. There may be other clues. They may complain more that their clothes are scratchy. They don't like surprises, they startle easily and don't like noisy places.

So how can you help a shyer child?

- Avoid excusing a more cautious child as 'shy' in front of other people so it does not turn into a self-fulfilling prophecy, and the child adopts this as a fixed label. With sensitive handling, which does not reinforce this tendency, as well as good role modelling from you, children who are initially shy as babies become more outgoing.

- Explain to your child that he may like to take things slowly and get used to things at his own pace to get the point across that he will eventually come out of his shell.

- In his early days, be his secure base from which to explore the world. As a toddler, introduce him to others from the safety of your arms so he can observe his surroundings and get used to his surroundings first.

- Take your child with you when you go out, so he gets to practise meeting others in smaller groups and quieter places. Find small local groups that offer movement, singing or drama activities to help him find his voice.

Most of all, don't see shyness in childhood as a major hurdle. Research has found that shy children tend to have just as many friends as more confident children. It's just that they may take a little more time to warm up, and their friendship circle a little longer to grow. In any case, it's only relatively recently, since the start of the twentieth century, that there's been a bias in our society towards louder and more extrovert personalities. Now the wheel is turning full circle. Those with socially sensitive temperaments are now increasingly recognised in the work-place, among other places, as having important qualities such as making more considered decisions, listening and understanding their peers better.

What is social IQ?

Some children come into the world with a natural aptitude for maths. Others arrive with a predisposition for art or writing. There is a reason why our strengths can shine in so many different ways. That's because intelligence has been found to be more than just a simple, one-dimensional IQ score.

Psychologists now believe there are many different types of intelligence and the leader in this field, Howard Gardner, has identified more than eight. Many are ones you might expect, like logical-mathematical, musical and linguistic. However, others include interpersonal skills – the ability to sense other people's feelings, and intrapersonal – the ability to understand yourself. People who measure highly in these two areas are better at relating to others, saying the right thing, reading body language correctly and understanding what makes other people tick.

As brain researcher Lise Elliott says in her book *Early Intelligence*: 'Emotion is every bit as much a function of the brain as intelligence. Yet we tend to focus more on developing intelligence, believing we can alter a child's achievement, when that is just as true of emotion.

'Our emotional and social lives are governed by the large set of neural structures known as the limbic system. Like every other part of the brain, a child's limbic system is moulded through the dual influence of nature and nurture. Each child is born with his or her own emotional make-up or temperament. But this innate bent is acted on by the unique environment in which a child is reared by parents and siblings.'

As we shall see in Part Three, even if they are not born with natural social ability, in the same way that a child with less aptitude for numbers can still learn algebra, a child with poorer social skills can also learn to make and keep good friends.

PART THREE
HOW TO HELP YOUR CHILD MAKE AND KEEP FRIENDS

'Tom has always struggled with friendships. As the years in infant school went by, he found it harder and harder to make friends. He was often told he couldn't play with other children because there wasn't "room" in their game. So we made great efforts to try to help by having kids back for tea every week. But the friendships were always short-lived before the other children either lost interest – or Tom moved onto someone else he thought was going to be his new friend. A typical boy, he would try to show off to make other kids laugh, but often it backfired. The other children saw jokes as annoying, alienating him further from the groups he was so desperate to be accepted into.'

Nicky, 40, a mother-of-two

'It's heart-breaking when my son Jonathan gets to know a child a little and then the other child distances themselves from him. This has happened a lot in his relationships with other boys. For example, Jonathan keeps asking a certain child for a sleepover but the boy is never interested. How do I explain that to him when he sees other kids pairing off for playdates after school?'

Christine, 43, mother-of-two

'My daughter Issy is a real trooper, so she covered up how she was being treated at school. She doesn't know why children don't play with her. She says nobody will include her in games. She told me she recently sat in the toilet all through break time because she didn't want others to see she had no one to spend it with.'

Giovanna, 49, mother-of-two

It's the first day of nursery. Children in spotless trainers and shiny backpacks are led to meet teachers, who lean over to fix sticky name labels on them and introduce themselves in sing-song voices.

But if these children are nervous as they step into this brand new world, the parents leading them in are even more so. It's clear from the hawkish way they watch from the sidelines that they know what this moment means.

Of course, any child can have first day nerves. Whether a youngster immediately moves towards a play table to strike up a conversation with a new classmate, or hovers nervously, unsure of what to say or do could be a clue as to how he easily he will navigate the Friendship Maze over the next 14 years of his education.

By the time children start school, a combination of temperament, brief life experience and how close they feel to the adults in their world, will help decide how this first day goes.

Until recently, it's been assumed that some children are just better at making friends than others. Yet in the same way as some children arrive on the planet with an instinctive eye for art, or a remarkably good ear for music, some children will be better than others at reading social cues.

By the age of three or four, while many are able to understand when to join in with another child's play, others stare wide-eyed not knowing what to do or say to enter the world of their peers. While it takes the average youngster less than a second to read another's social signals, for some youngsters it can take a little longer. According to a study by Atlanta's Emory University, roughly 10 per cent of children have problems understanding non-verbal signals. In a class of 30 children of any age, that means up to three of them will be uncertain of what to do, unless they are given a little extra help to decode them.

This may be one of the reasons scientists have found it relatively easy to band children by social position in classrooms – as we heard about in the previous part – and why there often seems to be a small group of outsiders in every class who tend to suffer socially.

The result is that, without adult intervention and guidance, such children can be viewed as 'annoying' or 'weird', sticky labels that can be difficult to peel off.

One such child is nine-year-old Edward. There's something about Edward's body language – and the way he 'hovers' at the edge of games but doesn't join in – that makes his classmates uncomfortable.

From time to time, Edward also pipes up with 'funny' things at unexpected times in lessons. His teacher recently complained at parents' evening that he started volunteering where he was going on holiday in the middle of a maths class.

Behind his back, other children complain too that Edward is a 'show-off' and a 'know-all' because he talks 'at' them, instead of listening to what they say.

So at break time, Edward often finds he has no one to play with. He sits on the fringes of the playground with a book, plays with younger children who are more likely to accept him, or asks to go the school library.

For Edward's mother, Amanda, it's painful to watch. Looking back now she can trace the first signs back to toddlerhood when she noticed Edward wasn't interacting the way other children did. Having missed out on these building blocks of social skills, her son didn't get the practice he needed and became more and more isolated from his peers.

Amanda says: 'Because Edward is bright, I used to think he was just grown-up for his age – and preferred talking to adults – and that he'd grow out of it.

'But now it's so heart-breaking to see him being left out of all the parties I know are happening in Year Four. He tells me he prefers adults and he doesn't care what people think of him, but I feel like I am a failure too. I worry for his future as well. Children this age can be very judgemental – and once you get labelled as strange, it's hard to escape that tag.'

Nor is it just boys. Girls can also suffer if they don't have a good working understanding of how the rules of friendship work.

Kathy Koenig, associate research scientist at the Yale Child Study Centre, says: 'For girls, socialization is all about communication, all about social-emotional relationships – discussions about friendship, who likes who and who doesn't like who and who is feuding with whom.' Some girls, however, don't 'get it' – and so when they realise they are failing, yet don't understand why, they can feel very isolated.'

Here's how to help. First of all, before we begin, what are the skills every child needs to make and maintain friendships in the first place? According to the seminal work of child psychologist Dr Michael Thompson, who has spent decades researching children's relationships, at any age they need to have the following abilities to make and keep friends:

- **Enjoy being with other people, whether with a special friend or a larger group**

- **Understand other people's feelings, read their emotions and be able to imagine what it's like to be them**

- **Manage anger and uncomfortable feelings like frustration and jealousy**

- **Trust that other people will like them and will remember them even when they are not with them**

- **Say sorry when they've hurt a friend's feelings.**

Yet even if these abilities don't come naturally, we can help children develop them.

According to Michelle Garcia Winner, one of the pioneers of social skills teaching in the US, children can practise by thinking about how others view them. By using their eyes, ears and brains, they can become 'social detectives' to learn what is expected from them. In other words, by teaching kids to look for clues in others' behaviour and to learn to look at themselves from other people's perspectives, children can start to work out how to get their message across, and ultimately communicate better.

Parent educator Noel Janis-Norton, who also teaches parents about social thinking skills told me: 'Luckily the brain is very malleable. Whenever we learn, we are changing the brain. It can be as simple as teaching kids the best way to use eye contact in social situations – or what body language to use in the playground. For example, many of these kids will be left on the fringes of games because they will be looking away from the group they want to be part of, instead of registering their interest. Teaching kids to turn their body and shoulders towards the group can be enough to let others know they want to be accepted.'

Part of the approach is to teach these children that if they act in ways that makes others feel awkward – like speaking at the wrong times, talking too long about certain subjects, or butting in at the wrong times – others will avoid them.

How to help improve your child's social skills

'When my little boy goes to primary school, he doesn't seem to understand why it's a good idea to say hello or look other people in the eye. When I ask him to, the other children are immediately more open to him or ask him to sit with them. But it doesn't come naturally to him and generally he says he prefers to play by himself.'
Fatima, 27, mother-of-one

'I always make sure my seven-year-old son is up with all the things that others boys are into, so he's got lots to talk about with other kids, but they still seem to ignore him. If he goes up to them in the playground, they turn their backs and tell him go away. I just can't understand it.'

Stella, 36, mother-of-one

'My daughter Emily was a child who could never find friends at school, often because she was too domineering. I did my best to help her see where she was going wrong. I had to email other mothers to invite her for play-dates because she'd see all the other kids go off with each other after school, and feel left-out. The summer before secondary school started, I decided enough was enough. We got some friendship skills cards which helped her think about how she was coming across to others. When she went into Year 7, she was able to turn over a new leaf. When she was helped to understand how her behaviour came across to others, she was able to start making good friends.'

Elaine, 45, mother-of-two

- **Talk about friendship:** For most of us, friendship is something intangible. We take it for granted that our interaction with our friends will be comfortable and easy. But some kids may need to think more deeply about what it means to be a friend – and what qualities make others want to spend time with them, like listening, sharing and understanding their point of view. Make a point of noticing and complimenting your child when they show these qualities. Talk too about your friendships – times when you have been a good friend by being thoughtful, dependable and ready to listen, and mention when others are a good friend to you, so they know how to be a good friend to others.

- **Train your child how to view the world from other people's perspectives:** This ability is an essential component of friendship that enables key skills like compromise, listening and sharing. Get your child into the habit of stepping into other people's shoes in everyday life. For example, ask your child: 'How does your friend feel now he has broken his toe and can't play football?' or 'Do you think your aunt is looking forward to starting her new job next month?'

- **Play turn-taking games:** Play games to practise cooperation. As you play board or ball games, describe out loud what you are doing. Start with non-competitive games, so younger children can get used to the to-and-fro of turn-taking first. As they build up their impulse control and tolerance, role model how to be a good loser by explaining that no one can win all the time, and next time there might be a different outcome. If your child does have a melt-down after losing, say: 'I know you were upset that you lost the game. But it's just a game and it's more fun if you learn how to manage your emotions. Is there anything you could do next time that won't ruin it for everyone and keep it fun?' Brainstorm solutions. Children learn best when they are asked to search their brains for the answers, rather than being told what to do.

- **Eat together:** Gathering around a table to eat is about much more than simply sharing a meal. Experts who analysed the eating habits of more than 24,000 children, aged six to eleven, found they had better social skills if they regularly sat around the table with their families. The experience gives them the chance to practise taking turns listening, sharing ideas and expanding conversation. It can be any meal so make these occasions as regular as you can – and make it a rule to put phones away.

- **Help your child name their emotions:** Even for adults, feelings can seem like a confusing maelstrom. It may help your child to understand their emotions better if they know that psychologists believe there are just four basic ones – joy, sadness, anger and fear. Everything is a mixture of these. There are other words which will help, if they know how to use them, too, like confused, surprised, disappointed, silly, uncomfortable, worried, lonely, shy or ignored, as well as positive emotions. Simply being able to find adjectives to describe how they feel will help your child to feel MORE in control. Talk too about times when you felt frustrated, resentful or envious and how you handled those feelings.

- **Model resolution:** When we argue with our partners, our children will be watching us closely. For the sake of your child (and of course your relationship) show them how to resolve your own disagreements with your partner – because there is no better way to teach conflict resolution. First listen to what your partner is saying, step away and take a few minutes to calm down if you feel your emotions are starting to overwhelm you. Reflect back what your partner is saying so they know you have understood and taken it on board. Even if you don't agree, summarising their grievance will take the heat out of many rows, because the other person knows they have been heard. Work out together how to address the issue – and finally say sorry for saying anything hurtful or ill-considered, without casting blame on them for 'making' you say it. If kids see us able to resolve conflicts – and take responsibility for our behaviour – they are more likely to mirror this behaviour in their own social relationships.

- **Try friendship cards:** Friendship cards (finkcards. co.uk) can be a good way to get children thinking about how to make friends and have healthy friendships.

They include questions like: 'How does your friend show you they are listening to you?' and 'How would you know if someone wanted to be your friend?'

Other everyday ways to help your child improve social skills

While every child will be a better friend if their parents develop the general techniques described in the last section, some youngsters will need longer-term practice to fine-tune their social skills.

- **Teach body language:** Explain to your child how body language affects the way others see us. Play games to show how this works. For example, turn off the sound on a TV programme or film and ask your child to guess what the characters are thinking. You could also take a video of your child, or look in the mirror, to help them work out what messages their body language and facial expressions are giving off. Show them how they will need to turn the front of their body towards a group to let others know they are interested in being friendly.

- **Show how facial expressions work:** Make a collage of photos of people making different faces and talk about what they mean. You could also practise making expressions with your child in the mirror, and talking about the messages they create. Help your child be conscious of the faces they pull too, by saying things like: 'That's a deep frown. It looks to me like you're worried about something.'

- **Make eye contact:** Set a good example by making eye contact when you speak to your child, and not looking at your phone. Explain that if they don't use their eyes to look at people, others will think they are not being friendly. Help get your child into this habit, by asking them the eye colour of the people they have talked to.

- **Practise tone of voice:** Tone is also an important part of conveying meaning. The tone a child might use to talk to his teacher, for example, will be different from the one they use with a peer. Show and practise how different voice inflections can be used to make a sentence like 'Can you please bring me the book?' sound either angry or polite. Read to them from books with lots of dialogue and get them to read to you. Audio books can also help youngsters understand different ways words can be said.

- **Teach them to match the tone:** Children can also practise how to be in tune with their peers' conversations. Explain how each conversation is a like a song – and it's best to avoid a sudden wrong note. This means that if a group of children come out of a test, saying how difficult it was, your child should not pipe up to say they found it ridiculously easy. This is not about teaching them to lie, but thinking of something to say that is sensitive to the way their peers feel.

- **Practise conversation:** Explain the importance of waiting for a reply and listening carefully to the answers in a conversation. Video your conversations so you can point out to your child what he's doing right, like smiling at the right moment, taking turns before responding and looking at the other person in the eye. It helps if this sort of activity is done on a regular basis, so try and set aside some time to practise these skills one-on-one, every day, and make it fun.

- **Recognise stop signals:** One of the main reasons children get labelled 'weird' is because they don't know when to stop – or think it's funny to continue doing something, like kicking the back of a classmate's chair or prodding them, to get a reaction. In a conversation, they may also go on about a subject long after the other child has lost interest – or repeatedly ask the same question until they get the answer they want. Show them how to read the body language signals that another child has lost interest, like looking elsewhere or turning their bodies away. Demonstrate too how to spot signs of irritation and anger in others' faces, like frowning or eye-rolling – and to take responses like 'Stop it' seriously the first time. Some children may also need to be told that repeating an annoying behaviour until it gets a reaction doesn't make it more amusing.

- **Take it slowly:** At first, keep play-dates on the shorter side, as children who struggle socially can find it tiring to have to remember so many new skills, as well as keep a lid on their emotions. The aim is for both your child and their guest to reach the end, having had a good time.

- **Show them how to join in:** One of the most painful moments for parents is watching their younger children forlornly standing on the edges of a game, not knowing how to join in. This too may need practice. For example, you may need to demonstrate how it's important for them to look, and turn their bodies and shoulders towards the group, as well as smile, to show they'd like to be included. Social scientists have found that rather than saying: 'Can I come into your game?' a direct question which can elicit a 'no', it works better for a child to show quiet interest, observe and see where they can slip in. It's also easier to pair up with a child on their own who will be glad of a playmate, or to join slightly larger groups of more than three. Help children think of ways they can contribute by coming up with a new role which would add to the game. Make it clear that not all their attempts will work and not to feel personally rejected. Sometimes other youngsters may be so wrapped up in their games they don't want an interruption.

- **Role-play:** The best way for children to learn these skills is for them to try them for themselves in a safe context at home. Try role playing different social scenarios with them – or giving them practice with same-age children, like cousins, who may be more tolerant and invested in keeping a game going.

- **Work on introductions:** Every friendship begins with a sign that two people are interested in each other. But children make snap judgements – and first impressions can last a long time. If another child makes a friendly approach, and yours responds by looking away or not talking back, they can get stuck with a 'weird' or 'rude' label. Before your child is in a situation where they have to meet new people, particularly at the start of a new school, rehearse those first introductions in a relaxed, unpressured way. If they still feel shy, suggest they smile and have a few simple questions ready. It won't necessarily lead to a close friendship, but it will prevent them being ruled out at the first hurdle. Teaching children basic courtesy in their dealings with others gives them an immediate advantage. As well as modelling manners yourself, give them practice interacting with others by asking them to greet guests, chat to shop staff or ring up and make appointments. Even if they don't get it exactly right, praise every little step in the right direction.

- **Read books:** Reading before bedtime is one of the most important times of the day for parents and children to connect and talk. It's also a proven way to help teach your child to understand others. In one experiment, researchers split a group of just over 100 children around the age of seven into two groups. Both sets were read the same illustrated story. One group were asked to draw a picture afterwards. The other was asked to talk about what happened between the characters. Two months later it was found that the group who talked about the story showed more empathy, and a better understanding of others than the other group who had not talked about it.

- **Get practice:** Look under 'Teaching Social Skills' on YouTube for videos to help your child practice. Other resources include 'The Social Detective' app which uses real-life video clips to help children read social cues and judge how to respond best.

What children find annoying about each other

'I got friendly with a mother in Year Four who had moved her daughter from another primary because the other children left her out. It wasn't long before she was complaining that the same thing was happening again. When I asked my daughter why, she said the new girl always insisted everyone played the games she wanted. If they didn't, she'd sulk. The other classmates went along with it for a while, but then soon they got fed up with her kicking off and she was left on her own again. To adults, the child looks lovely and polite, so the mum was utterly baffled.'
Maryam, 33, mother-of-one

> *'I asked my son what makes other children annoying. In no particular order, he said showing off, being too rough — like shoving and pushing — telling people what games to play and getting really angry when a game doesn't go their way.'*
>
> **Sophie, 32, mother-of-one**

> *'My son is eight and he would love a best friend. But the fact that he always wants to dictate what games to play puts other children off. He doesn't seem to understand conversation is a two-way street. He talks for a long time about himself and doesn't pay attention to what the other children say back.'*
>
> **Richard, 47, father-of-one**

Children who have weaker social skills often find it harder to see themselves as others do – or understand the impressions they make. Often they do not have a clue where they are going wrong, which means they end up making the same mistakes again and again. If you feel your child could do with some targeted help, observe their interactions more closely. Watch them in the playground, quietly monitor play-dates and talk to teachers and other parents to decide how they could be helped. By identifying the issues, and gently making your child aware, you can help remove some of the barriers standing in the way of their friendships.

Being a 'show-off'
Children may brag in the mistaken belief that if others look up to them, they will be impressed and like them more. Some may not yet understand that, on the contrary, it sounds like they're showing off. Whether it's through role-play, or talking about your own experiences, explain to your child he will gain more friends by looking for the common ground he has with others, rather than trying to look more superior.

Being a 'bad sport'
It does not take much for children to go off a child who cheats in games, argues about the rules, has a strop when they lose or brags too much when they win. For youngsters of every age, the first priority is having fun, so they would rather exclude anyone who might ruin that. Put the experience of losing in context for your child by pointing out that no one wins all the time. Go to YouTube and find examples of sporting role models losing with good grace. Explain how winning and losing is temporary. The key point is for your child to enjoy themselves during a game, not to get hung up on the outcome.

Being 'gross'
There are acts – like nose-picking or bottom scratching – which are always considered disgusting in public. As they grow up, most children quickly pick up on what these are and develop the self-restraint not to do them. However some children are slower to understand how such habits are viewed by others, and that their peers may not want to be friends with them as result. They may not realise that unsavoury behaviour only has to be witnessed a few times by classmates before a child gets branded with a reputation for being 'gross'.

It's possible your child may not notice what they are doing and their behaviour has become an unconscious habit. Ask your child if he's noticed if there are times, when he's concentrating, lost in thought, or nervous, when he is more likely to pick his nose. Question how he thinks it looks to others, and get him to register when he feels the urge to do it again. If he has got stuck in a phase, find an alternative activity that will give him another kind of sensory satisfaction, like squeezing a stress ball or stroking his nose. Explain that using a tissue will mean his behaviour won't be viewed as so disgusting. Check too though that your child isn't suffering from an allergy which is also irritating the lining of his nose.

Make him aware at home, too. No matter how old your child is, when you see him do it, quietly take his hand, without telling him off, give him a tissue and ask him to wash his hands. Another way to cut back on the habit is to apply Vaseline to the inside of the nostrils. The slippery feeling will take away the satisfaction of nose-picking, and also moisturise the membranes that may have become damaged and itchy, and which may have kept him returning to the habit.

Being a cry-baby

Every day children are involved in small dramas, conflicts and differences of opinion. One way youngsters can make others wary of them is by being disproportionately touchy and oversensitive when these happen. It means that other youngsters will feel they can never relax and have fun with them – in case your child takes something they say or do the wrong way. If they keep flaring up, your child may find that others steer clear of them and don't invite them to play-dates and parties.

If you think this is happening, some children may need special coaching from adults on how to see others' behaviour in context and respond appropriately. Help them stay more reasonable by generally encouraging them to assume the best, not the worst, about others' motives. For example, just because two of your son's teammates at football are laughing together doesn't mean they are joking about him. They could just have discovered something in common to laugh about. He shouldn't jump to negative conclusions.

You may also have to talk through with your child, how it's not possible to control how others act or behave. He can only control how he responds.

Spell out how others will respect, listen and want to be around him much more if he keeps his temper. Give specific praise too, when he manages to stay calm or recovers quickly in challenging situations with other family members, so he knows when he's getting it right.

Being a tell-tale

As parents we want kids to be guided by our rules and tell us if there's anything that's worrying them. But if your child tells on their peers every time they spot a rule being broken, other children won't want to have them around. Children who crave adult validation to be seen as particularly well-behaved or perfect may also do this – and can become unpopular. Your goal here is for your child to be more selective about what they tell adults. Suggest they ask themselves: 'Is someone going to get hurt? Is anyone crying? Is someone being bullied?' If the answer is no, explain they won't need to tell an adult any more, and should allow other children to work out for themselves the right thing to do because it's important they apply the rules for themselves.

How to foster children's out-of-school relationships

While it's important not to overload children, and to give them downtime to get to know themselves, a well-chosen, after-school activity or camp in the school holidays can help extend a child's social circle.

When things get tough in school, it's also reassuring to have friends with common interests who are not part of the rigid classroom hierarchy. It means what happens in school does not have to be the be-all and end-all – and reminds children there are others out there who share their passions.

Common interests and hobbies are very much the glue that binds children's friendships. If you can find some that build on your child's innate, natural interests, they have a better chance of finding a mate with whom they have a lot in common – and the friendship will get off to a flying start. If your child is under-confident with her relationships, it may help to build up her competence in other areas. It's easier now there are so many more creative choices for out-of-school activities, ranging from computer coding to DJ'ing.

The easiest way to find an activity your child will love – and where they will meet like-minded people – is to select it according to their 'spark'. The concept, which sounds deceptively simple, was developed by the late youth development worker Peter Benson. He explained: 'Every child has a spark – something that is good, beautiful and useful to the world ... A spark is something that illuminates a young person's life and gives it energy and purpose.'

Sparks can be musical, athletic, intellectual, academic or relational and consist of anything from helping to save animals, playing an instrument, taking part in a sport or growing and making things.

Sparks are split into three types: a skill or talent your child is naturally good at, a commitment such as volunteering or helping the world, or a quality of character, such as empathy or being a good listener. A spark is always linked to an innate talent because kids like to do things that come easily to them. Finding their spark helps youngsters use their time better and feel good about themselves. It can be used to help your child become more fulfilled, and better choose how she uses her time. It might also eventually help light their way to a more satisfying career.

To discover your child's spark, all you have to do is ask your child what they love to do when they have the freedom to do it – and when they are away from social media and video games. Eight out of ten twelve-year-olds will already have a good idea straight away.

If your child is still too young to work it out for themselves, watch how they play. Keep an eye out for the activities that totally absorb them and that they do when they are alone. Getting a chance to meet children with the same shared passion will help them bond with less effort – and help overcome any social awkwardness. Try it out first, and look for one without too much formal structure or adult interference, so kids can really interact. If they hate it or have to be forced to go, leave it. If it's their spark, they are likely to take to it right away and be more interested in the other people who share it too.

How to help a child who says: 'Nobody likes me'

All children will say this from time to time. But if it's a repetitive complaint, it could be a sign there is a problem to address or they are starting to think they are unlikeable. Over time, these youngsters may have internalised the micro-aggressions and exclusions of other children. If this negative self-talk goes on uncontradicted, these voices can grow louder. Step in before they do more long-term damage to your child's self-worth – as this make them easier targets for bullying. It's the children who already bully themselves who are the most likely to be bullied by others.

Challenge 'never and always' thinking: Challenge them to be more realistic in their appraisal of themselves, and adjust their thinking to help shrink their problems back to their real size. Help them to see when they are overgeneralising ('I said a stupid thing in science and now everyone thinks I'm an idiot') and 'catastrophising', or blowing things out of proportion ('My friend didn't save me a seat at lunch, so I wonder if she secretly hates me.')

And finally...

One of the traits that makes children most liked by their peers is a sense of humour. Surprisingly, social scientists have found this is a characteristic that can be encouraged, and is mostly taught by parents in the home. So keep it light at home, laugh about things that go wrong, and keep up an upbeat family atmosphere to enjoy your time with your child. Their peers will appreciate it too.

How to help every child become strong enough to deal with friendship issues

Take a browse through the social media pages of tweens and teenagers and they look confident, brazen even. They pose, pull faces and show off for the camera. After all, by the age of thirteen they are already masters of their own universe, as they project their own idealised avatars into cyberspace. Scratch the surface though, and you may find it's not real confidence, but something more brittle: bravado borrowed from pop videos and celebrity culture.

In fact, statistics on depression, anxiety and self-harm show our children are more vulnerable than their exteriors suggest.

From every direction, youngsters are inundated with messages that they have to work harder, be popular, well-dressed and look good. Advertisers, the internet, magazines, the fashion industry and television get children hooked by telling them they are simply not good enough, hot enough or cool enough.

If their self-worth is eroded by these messages, they may trade off other children to feel better about themselves, or seek more approval from their peers.

The good news is that the best defence against assaults on their self-worth is you, the parent. It's family life that develops self-acceptance and competence, separate from the values which are celebrated on social media.

Here are just some of the benefits your child will reap from your efforts to actively build their inner core:

- They will know themselves well enough to be able to brush off and fight off put-downs. If they are bullied, they will know it's not their fault

- They won't be as desperate for the approval of their peer group in everything they do or wear

- They won't believe they are defined by what they own or wear

- They will choose friends who are worthy of them and will choose healthy relationships over unhealthy ones

- They will forgive themselves when things go wrong and get back up again.

HOW TO HELP

- **Help kids feel capable:** The more self-worth children have, the less swayed they are by the opinions of others – and the less they will need peer approval to feel good about themselves. Parents can help build this, but not by repeatedly telling kids how wonderful or special they are. Self-worth comes from feeling competent. So whether it's putting up a tent by themselves, helping with some DIY or showing them how they can teach themselves to play the guitar, foster opportunities where children can develop skills and talents by themselves. When your child feels self-worth from a range of tangible accomplishments, they will have more confidence to deal with friendship challenges. Armed with this core of self-belief, they will have less need to put others down in order to make them feel better about themselves.

- **Help them find what they are good at**: Adolescents, who are trying to forge their identities, are always looking for what sets them apart or makes them feel special. As they are constantly comparing themselves to others, it helps if they know they have a skill or talent which wins respect from their peers. Once they have discovered their 'spark' (as we've already discussed on page 129), it underpins their confidence and stops them searching for less healthy ways of feeling special or powerful. It's easier now as there are so many creative choices for out-of-school activities, whether it's coding, skateboarding or drama. So pay attention to what your child is good at and help them find ways to pursue their natural talents and interests.

- **Celebrate your child's uniqueness**: There's no child in the world the same as yours. So enjoy the combination of qualities that make your son or daughter who they are. Help kids tell their own personal stories of their journey with photographs they like – and have also taken – in scrapbooks. At the same time give them a secure base of family rituals, and celebrations.

THE BOTTOM LINE: **Teach children a growth mindset.** By their teenage years, children can feel trapped and hopeless, if they believe they have no control to change themselves or the world around them. Because they don't yet have the benefit of perspective or the autonomy of an adult, they tend to think that how it is now is how it will always be. As they get older, this can develop into feelings of low mood or, at worst, depression. Yet one of the greatest gifts you can give a child is the belief that they always have the power to improve themselves and their situation. That includes friendships. If they find these relationships difficult,point out that they can always get better at social skills and learn to understand themselves, and others, better. Assure them that they will make many good friends over their lifetime – and they only need a couple of good ones at any one time to feel happy and accepted.

How to help children to open up

'In general, I don't tell my parents anything unless it's a really big problem that the school will tell them about. I don't want them to be worried about me.'
Nathaniel, 15

'When I was checking my daughter's phone, I found the number for an anti-bullying helpline. It turned out she was being bullied by the Little Miss Perfect in the class. She had been too embarrassed to tell me and begged me not to say anything. She was certain if the girl got told off, she'd get her back by getting other people to turn against her.'

Sonia, 31, mother-of-one

'I thought my daughter's relationship with her best friend was all fine. It was only after the other girl left at the end of term that it all came out how mean and controlling she could be. She was so scared of being on her own, she put up with it. My daughter didn't want to tell me anything because she was embarrassed.'

Annette, 43, mother-of-three

'How was school today?'
'OK'
'What did you do at break-time?'
'Nothing much.'
'Who did you sit with at lunch?'
'Can't remember.'

These are the sorts of answers many of us get when we ask our children how their day went.

One of the reasons children's social lives are such a mystery is that they grant us less and less access as they get older, particularly in the secondary school years. Of course, it's a natural part of growing up for youngsters to confide more in their peers than their parents, as they move towards adulthood.

Boys in particular can be especially secretive because, as we've seen, they are conditioned to believe that showing weakness is not a typically masculine quality. All this means, however, is that when things do go wrong, parents find themselves shut out and unable to give the benefit of an adult perspective.

Furthermore, our children are so desperate to make us proud of them, they often feel ashamed when things have spun out of control.

Rows with friends are also rarely black and white. Your child is unlikely to be completely innocent when relationships veer off track. At some point, they know full well they will have said or written something that will show them in a bad light which they don't want us to know about.

They may also fear that if a friendship issue has flared up, we will pour petrol over the flames of an already difficult situation. They fear if we hear about a conflict, we won't understand, we will wade in, we will start demanding meetings with teachers or contacting other parents.

Worse still, we might take away their phones and iPads, which are their lifelines. Even when they are being hurt at every turn, young people are obsessed with what's being said about them – and are desperate to be able to monitor and respond.

Of course, they are the ones who have to face their peers at school day in and day out, not us. In their minds, the ideal would be for the whole problem to just magically disappear. It means that in the increasingly fraught social lives our children now lead, they can get enmeshed in serious problems which can lead to low moods or self-harm – and often parents are none the wiser.

- **Pick your moment:** Imagine spending all day at work, and being told you had to be on your best behaviour at every moment – or face a severe ticking off. In each task you are set, you must excel. Then, no matter how well you have performed, you get to take even more work home at the end of the day. This is not something any adult would put up with. Yet after a school day like this, children have grown-ups waiting at the door to grill them about how it went. Even though our interest comes out of a place of love, not surprisingly, many don't want a performance review the moment they come home. Furthermore, the more pressured and test-based the school system becomes, the more time kids need to decompress. If you want to show your interest in their lives, actions speak louder than words. When you first see your child after school, welcome them warmly, say you missed them and give them a hug. (Scientists have found that a good long hug is enough to boost levels of the feel-good hormones oxytocin for hours afterwards.) By not asking a young person for a full debrief, unless they want to give one, they will feel you love them unconditionally, irrespective of how they've done at school that day. This, in turn, will make them less guarded. They will relax more around you, and be more open later, in the run-up to bedtime, when they are often more in the mood to talk. If you do have a question, make it: 'What made you laugh most today?'

- **Take any opportunity:** Even if it's late and you're tired and you have a hundred things on your to-do list, if your child wants to chat, grab the chance. They may even pick a time when you are busy to test you, and see how much you really care, so don't fail them. Look for other chances to talk every day, like the quiet times before bedtime, in the car on the way to activities or after lights out.

- **Don't interview for pain:** On the other hand, there are children who realise that describing a full-scale friendship drama is a sure-fire way to get your full attention. Some may enjoy having you as their champion. Others just want to pass you a 'hot potato' – and unload their problems to make themselves feel better. While of course we want to comfort our children, we also have to check our natural protectiveness does not blow the original issue out of proportion.

- **Understand their loyalty to their friends:** As they get into their teenage years, children become increasingly loyal to their friends, no matter what they've done, or how badly they are treated by them. In their own minds, they will also be weighing up how much of their social lives they now want to share with you, so it's worth recognising that you'll probably never get the whole story of what's happening in their friendship circle. If you're even getting half of it, you're doing well.

- **Don't expect to have the magic answers:** Relationships are complex and there are rarely quick fixes. Usually kids assume parents don't have much of a clue what really goes on in their world, but are looking for the chance to talk to someone they can trust. When they want to talk, usually just listening is enough. It's often what you don't say, rather than what you do, that will make you the best sounding board. Lend an empathetic ear instead. When children have issues, what they need most is an adult to listen to them, not a bouncer or lawyer.

THE BOTTOM LINE: *When your child does come to you with a real friendship problem, thank them for telling you - and listen. Restrain your judgements and prejudices and avoid coming out with pat reactions like: 'Just ignore it' (as your child has probably been trying to do this already) or 'They're just jealous of you' (this may make you feel better, but it doesn't help). If you get it wrong, your upset child will dismiss you with the words: 'I knew you wouldn't understand.'*

And if you have drifted apart...

The sheer pace of life means that adults these days often don't have enough time to keep the lines of communication open with their children. Although parents are usually 'around', the breakneck speed at which we now live – plus the fact there are more two-parent-working households than ever before – means that unless we are careful, our children can process this busyness as rejection.

The first signs can start to show sooner than you think. Children, who don't have the perspective to realise you work long hours to provide for them materially, may start to feel they are not important enough for you to spend time with. As early as seven or eight, they may begin to withdraw from you.

As they head towards the tween and teens years, these feelings of rejection may develop into in hypersensitivity, defensiveness or sulky behaviour. Too often, this can lead to a vicious circle in which young people get labelled and blamed for being 'difficult', by parents who find it hard to admit that the loss of connection with their child is a contributory factor.

At the same time as your relationship becomes more distant, your children's peers become more important to them – and your sway with them becomes less and less, particularly during the critical teenage years.

In order for children to be guided by parents – and for us to be able to step in and help out in tough times – they must feel close to us. They will be far more invested in listening to you, if you show you want to spend time with them, for no other reason other than you enjoy their company.

It sounds corny, but children really do spell the word 'love' as 'time' – and occasionally we need reminding that it's running out, and that their childhoods are only fleeting. From birth to the age of twelve, we have just 4,380 days with them. Yet sometimes we are so busy trying to give our children everything materially, we don't give them what they need most – us.

Many parents try to get by with an on-going promise that things will get better soon, but, as family educator Rob Parsons of Care for the Family points out: 'A slower day is not coming.' While it's true that you won't ever have more time, what you can do is prioritise what you do have. You can pay less attention to the things that don't really matter – like celebrity culture, gadgets and television – and spend more time on your children, who do.

The good news is that it is never too late to adjust the emotional temperature in your home – and the effects will be instantaneous. Putting boundaries around your work, placing limits on your technology use and taking steps to de-stress – all of these things will have an immediate effect on your relationship with your child.

Holding ordinary conversations, playing games, doing simple things together – like cooking and going for walks – are all you need to do. Nonetheless, it's time that needs to be set aside and dedicated to your child.

Other ways to get talking again

If your son never tells you about his feelings or friendship problems, it could be that, as a boy, no one has ever thought to share their feelings with him. If your daughter doesn't want to tell you she is unhappy with the way her best friend bosses her around, she may believe you don't have time to listen. When you're tired, after work or at weekends, it's tempting to be more concerned with tackling your to-do list than hear about what's happening in their friendship group. But unless you make time for your child, you will be adding to your workload.

If your relationship with your child has drifted off course, the first step is to recognise that they are likely to have become defensive and non-cooperative because they feel you do not want them around.

To reclaim your closeness, psychologist Oliver James recommends a technique called 'love bombing'. This involves spending a period of time alone with your child, offering them unlimited love and control over what you do, in order to re-establish the trust between you.

James believes that by taking your relationship back to its roots, you can stabilise the levels of the fight or flight hormone, cortisol, which gradually keeps rising when a child feels rushed or criticised, and which may send your child into a constant state of apprehension around you. The idea is that by freeing your child from being constantly controlled, it will take you back to the closeness and intimacy you once shared when they were young children, and before other issues gradually came between you. Of course, it sounds mad to give a child total freedom to set the rules, but it's only for a short space of time – usually a weekend – and children usually make perfectly reasonable requests. After a few days, parents can see dramatic results.

If your child seems to be morose about their social lives or, as we shall discuss, has been mean to other children, spending a few days with them may be the best first step to find out what's really going on. It's only by spending time on re-forging your bond, that your child will feel comfortable enough to open up – and let you in to help.

No matter how low they feel, they are never alone.

THE BOTTOM LINE: *As we've heard, children will sometimes talk about the things that bother them and sometimes they won't. Wherever they are on this spectrum, give them the baseline message: If they are ever in trouble, danger, ill or mentally overwhelmed, they can always come to you. That applies even if they think no one can help, or adults won't understand. Tell them to give you a chance anyway. It takes an adult to know that time heals – and today is not forever.*

PART FOUR
HOW TO HELP YOUR CHILD HANDLE SOME OF THE MOST COMMON FRIENDSHIP PROBLEMS

So far, we've looked at how and why children's friendships have changed, and why some find it harder to make friends than others. By bringing together the latest research around children's social lives, I hope you feel you now have a map to better understand the twists and turns. This final part is to help your child get back on track at the times when they lose their way.

Relational aggression between girls

When Alexa walks into the classroom on her non-school-uniform day in Year Seven, she takes one look at her friend Lottie's carefully chosen outfit and says: 'Nice shirt!' with a withering look. She then walks off, leaving Lottie lost in a whirlpool of confusion, not sure what to do or say.

In Year Three, Annabel spots Lisa whispering about her to her friend, Eve, at break time. Later that day, Eve informs her she only wants to play with Lisa today – and the two girls sit together at lunch without saving Annabel a seat. Tearful and confused, Annabel torments herself wondering what Lisa could have said about her – or what she could have possibly done wrong.

Until relatively recently, our main concerns have been the physical attacks and intimidation of traditional bullying. But then, over the last decade, social scientists and educators have homed in on a much more hidden kind of social conflict. It's relational aggression, a kind of stealth attack, using words and exclusion. It happens between children in the same classrooms and friendship group and takes a slightly different form in girls and boys because of the way they relate to each other.

In girls, it has its own special character because our daughters are not supposed to engage in open conflict – they are expected to 'be nice to each other'. It means that aggression gets driven underground into name-calling, seat-saving, gossip and blanking.

According to Rachel Simmons, who has written widely on relational aggression: 'Unlike boys who tend to bully acquaintances or strangers, girls frequently attack between tightly knit networks of friends, making aggression harder to identify and intensifying the damage to targets.'

Because girls value closeness and secret-sharing, they not only make great friends, they also make fearsome enemies. In their intimate moments, they reveal so much of themselves to each other, that they are armed with all the ammunition they need. They already have an intimate knowledge of their opponents' weak spots.

Here the back-turning, glaring, note-passing and rumour-spreading is so subtle that most of it flies beneath the radar of parents and teachers. The power of relational aggression is that it's very difficult to spot, and is designed to be almost impossible to prove. It is deliberately designed to inflict psychological, rather than physical pain. For example, if Lottie had complained to a teacher about Alexa's shirt comment, Alexa could easily have claimed it was actually a compliment and Lottie would have been told to 'stop being so sensitive'.

However, if your daughter is on the receiving end, she may not want to admit it's happening – because she'd rather put up with being treated badly than be cast out of the friendship circle in which it is taking place.

This can leave parents at a loss, and unsure of what to do when their daughters come home in tears, feeling embarrassed or isolated. Often girls caught up in this type of situation will be tearful at home, find it hard to concentrate and will not want to go to school. It doesn't help that as relational aggression takes place among friends, our daughters will beg adults not to get involved, no matter how miserable it's making them.

So why do girls (although as we shall see, studies also show boys use relational aggression) – act so cruelly to one another? In a world in which popularity is now visible and measurable in the numbers of likes and friends on social media, the fight for the top spots has become more intense. In a more competitive culture of looks and academia, in which many young people feel they are not enough, it often feels more important than ever to win the approval and validation of peers – even if they have to climb over other people to get it.

The sharpening desire to be seen as socially powerful means allegiances can be formed and broken at dizzying speed. The most insecure, in particular, may be prepared to hurt and abandon their former allies to build their status.

While these power plays may not inflict physical wounds – and vary in severity – they should still be taken seriously. Never underestimate the terror of a child who has to go into a classroom every day, knowing she will be glared at or have no one to sit with at lunch, because she's been ostracised by her group.

So how do you spot relational aggression? One clue is that your child may have a roller-coaster relationship with certain friends. This is because when the other child, usually with the upper hand, senses they have gone too far, they will often pull back until yours is lulled into a false sense of security. After belittling them, they may change tack and start being nice again. By now the underdog is so grateful to no longer be in the frenemy's sights (a frenemy is someone a child stays friends with despite the nasty way they are treated), that some can become almost puppy-like in their submissiveness – to try and avoid being wounded again.

In other words, random and unpredictable meanness can be a good way to keep rivals and subordinates on their toes.

The Queen Bee, Alexa, described earlier, who stung her friend Lottie out of the blue with an attack on her outfit, was nice to her the next time she saw her. Deep down Alexa knows her friend is now scared of a repeat attack, which will be particularly stinging if it's witnessed by others. This way, Alexa strengthens her position within the group by making others afraid of her.

According to research compiled by The Ophelia Project, a non-profit organisation that aims to reduce this kind of conflict in schools, 48 per cent of students are regularly exposed to relational aggression. Yet by pinpointing these acts for what they are, talking about what a good and bad friend is, and by helping girls better understand the politics of their peer group, it's possible to limit its impact. While every child will experience it from time to time, we can help kids see it coming, identify it for what it is and draw protective boundaries around themselves.

Furthermore, training your daughter to recognise and walk away from these kinds of relationships can be viewed as a life skill. After all, you wouldn't want her to put up with a partner who puts her down when she starts to form her adult romantic relationships.

Types of relational aggression

- Alliance building against a target

- Name-calling, labelling and humiliation

- Exclusion (e.g. 'You can't sit here') and forming exclusive cliques

- Back-turning, silent treatment and ignoring

- Sighing/eye-rolling/tutting

- Threats or pressure (e.g. 'If you don't do this, I won't be your friend').

HOW TO HELP

- **Map out the dynamics:** With an understanding of what relational aggression is – and the roles of aggressors, targets and by-standers (those who watch and say nothing) within her peer group, your child will be better equipped to name what is happening, spot the patterns of behaviour and call out aggression for what it is.

- **Avoid it yourself:** Young people learn some of this behaviour from grown-ups. Don't sulk, ignore or use sarcasm with your child. When children learn first-hand how much these methods hurt, they can become their weapons of choice too.

- **Let her express anger:** As a society, we socialise girls to be, in the words of the nursery rhyme, 'sugar and spice and all things nice.' The message they get is that they have to be good girls; and that means being caring and passive. At home, let your daughter express her negative feelings. No emotion is wrong in itself, but feelings can be channelled in both healthy and unhealthy ways.

- **Show her how to question it:** It's important that your child also sends a message that she will not be a victim in order to protect her own sense of self. A simple challenge can be all it takes to nip this type of guerrilla attack in the bud. When an instigator says something unkind, show your child to call out the behaviour immediately with questions like: 'Can you repeat that?' or 'What do you mean?'. If the other child has a clear conscience, they won't mind answering the question. If their conscience is not clear, the originator will think twice about repeating it. If your child also witnesses this sort of behaviour among her friends, train her to label it on the spot too, so that there's zero tolerance in her friendship group. Otherwise instigators take the silence as tacit consent for what they are doing – and it will keep happening.

Relational aggression between boys: When does banter become bullying?

'I got a lot of comments about my height, like: "What's it like down there Lego-Man?"'
Leon, 11

As we've heard, one of the greatest challenges for parents when hearing about their children's relationships is working out what is normal interaction – and what crosses the line into cruelty.

Among boys it can be even harder to spot. For them, teasing is the glue that bonds friendship. Here a clever put-down is often considered an art form. If a boy gets an insult, his challenge is to top it with a more withering or witty riposte. Boys in the same friendship group can say things to each other that girls would never say to each other, except in the most vicious of fights. You only have to see the humiliation that men put each other through on their stag nights, to appreciate how even the most brutal humour can sometimes be used affectionately between males.

By secondary school, boys may call each other by such insulting names and use so much sarcasm that it may be hard to tell when teasing has become hurtful – and whether your son is starting to feel demeaned.

For a boy on the receiving end, the challenge is to show they can take it without looking ruffled or upset so he can stay in his gang. In boy-world, it's imperative that, just like Batman, if he wants to save face, he should never let his mask of inscrutability slip. If it drops, a boy will fear he's in for much worse teasing, particularly if it's from a boy higher up the social ladder.

This is all made more complicated by the fact that the teasers use various tactics to pull back from the brink, like pretending what they said was all 'a joke', or adding phrases like: 'Only messing with you'. No matter how hurt his feelings, your son will usually respond with 'No problem' rather than risk being seen as weak and sensitive.

However, when the teasing goes all one way, and is so regular that it turns into taunting, or crosses the line from humorous to humiliating, then he may need to say something.

The good news is that boys feel they have much more permission to be assertive than girls do. If your son is upset by constant remarks about his appearance, for example, discuss how he could simply and quickly put his feelings into words. Suggest he ask to speak to the main perpetrator alone, and tells him in a straightforward, direct way that he would like it to stop.

A boy's friends will know it takes a lot for a mate to say he's no longer finding the jokes funny any more. But by stating his grievance, if only for just a moment, he will make his point. Remember that boys don't like drama and fall-outs and tend to see them as something girls do, so most would rather back off than escalate tension. If done purposefully, your son will also win respect by setting his boundaries.

If he's teased by someone more powerful so that he looks vulnerable, and it's happening relentlessly, then teasing crosses the line into bullying. At that point, he may need the guidance of parents and teachers to deal with it, as outlined later in the book.

THE BOTTOM LINE: *Teasing makes up much of the interaction between boys, but there is a difference between 'good' teasing and 'bad' teasing. If a boy feels hurt, or that the person saying these things does not like him or just wants to push his buttons, help him to tell the instigator that he wants it to stop.*

Common reasons why friendships fracture

Whether your son or daughter is the doing the dumping, or has been dumped, it helps for everyone to look at their part. Did both friends invest as much time and energy? Did one often cancel arrangements at the last minute, when something better came along, making the other feel devalued? Did competition creep into their relationship? Did they just outgrow each other? Have they lost what they had in common?

These are all painful issues, but, whatever the answer, asking searching questions can help your child develop their emotional intelligence, and help them understand the factors that make friendship possible.

Beyond that, if your child has lots of friendship dramas, help them to spot repetitive patterns that keep cropping up – like possessiveness or oversensitivity. It's only by learning from mistakes, and realising what needs to change, that they can go on to have better relationships. Here are some of the most common reasons friendships fracture.

It's become one-sided: Friendships need to be equally reciprocal to thrive. If both parties don't put the same amount of time and effort into the relationship – or one starts to cancel arrangements or become flaky, it will start to falter. There has to be equal give and take.

It's become controlling: Some children want to control their friends to feel powerful. While at first your child may be flattered by the other's close attention, after a while they could start to feel manipulated and blackmailed into doing what the other wants, and they will want to break away.

They have moved in different directions: Adolescents can be like snakes shedding skins. Because friends are so important to their identity, they can be brutal about moving on.

It's become competitive: If one-upmanship seeps into any relationship, it means neither party can relax or can be truly honest with the other. Each will stop confiding in the other, fearing they may give away their advantage. As a result the intimacy and trust, the essence of a good friendship, gets lost.

It's about something else: It can save some heartache along the way if your child trains themselves to look under the superficial, mean words. So, for example, if your child and her former best friend become hostile towards each other when they are put in separate classes at the start of secondary school, scratch a little deeper. Now that they have been split up, are the pair locked in a race to prove who is the most popular? Does the child who feels he or she is losing the battle, feel the need to edge ahead again by spreading nasty rumours about the other? When a boy randomly ignores the best mate he's known since nursery school, is he being mean? Or actually, is he trying to save himself from the pain of separation when he goes to a different school next September? We can never really see into the minds of others, but if you try to do so in order to interpret their unpleasant behaviour more compassionately, there's generally no harm done.

HOW TO HELP

- **Role model emotional responsibility:** As the person who teaches your child the most about relationships, be the best role model you can. Do a 'rewind' on conflicts you have had. When talking about your own feelings, use 'I felt' statements to accept responsibility, rather than accuse. Tell them how you said sorry if you made mistakes. If you blame others, your child is likely to become a blamer too.

- **Be a rock:** Remember that your child is facing this break-up, knowing that their peers are watching. They may feel hurt, humiliated, angry and confused. Make time to listen, resist the urge to give advice and don't badmouth the former friend or ignore their parents, because you feel as if your child has been rejected. What you can give is your perspective – that we all have many different friends for different times in our lives – and moving on means your child now has room to find new companions.

> **THE BOTTOM LINE:** *The secret to being less stressed about human relationships is to bear in mind that you can't control or change other people's behaviour. You can only change your own.*

Helping your child move on

If your child is in a friendship that is not making them happy, naturally your first instinct is to want them to move away from the person you feel is undermining them.

But for a child stuck in close contact with their adversary day after day, in the closed setting of school, it's not that easy. At first, they may be in denial, or willing to put up with the mistreatment. That's because having a friend, who's nice some of the time, is better than risking being alone.

Of course, it will take a patient parent to stay silent, when your child is moaning bitterly about their frenemy one day and asking if they can go for a sleepover at their house the next.

This disengagement is a process. If we look back on our own relationship break-ups, we can see it takes time, even for adults.

To break away, your child has to find the answer inside themselves. Suggest they examine their gut feelings when they spend time with their friend. Do they feel uplifted when they see them – or nervous about what mood they will be in? Can they tell them everything? Or do they worry they can't confide in them? Eventually your child will work out for themselves that they would rather spend time with those who lift them, rather than put them down.

Be supportive but not overbearing. Whether it's taking the time to strike up a conversation with someone new at school – or sitting with a new lunch partner, youngsters deserve praise for every step they make in the right direction.

Gossip and rumour

'We're obsessed with talking about each other. As soon as one of us leaves the room, the rest of us talk about what that person just said.'
Maisy, 13

'I meet up with my best friend every Wednesday after school to bitch. We call it "Beef (social drama) Wednesday".'

Enya, 12

For young people, gossip is their currency. They use it to learn more about each other – to gauge the reaction of their friends on news of what their peers are up to, to discharge their jealous feelings and to reinforce group norms. At times when their self-worth is ebbing, gossip about someone else's mistakes can always make an insecure young person feel that little bit more superior.

Gossip starts to escalate as children's social relationships get more complicated, at the end of primary school. At this stage, the talk centres on who is friends with who, who's having a row and who's got a crush on who. By the start of secondary school, gossip gets bartered to build and take away social status. The scoop on someone else can be sold on to try and buy a place further up the social pecking order.

For example, a juicy nugget ('Did you hear what Karen said about you in art class?') may also be used curry favour with a more socially powerful friend. Like a stick of dynamite, the person who lights the fuse becomes the centre of attention. Reporting back to the subject is a way of a wannabe friend saying 'I'm on your side' and 'Reward me with attention for watching your back'.

By around Years 10 and 11, when social status is more settled, the most compelling gossip will have moved onto more adult themes: Who's dating who and who misbehaved most at the last party.

Yet when it backfires, gossip can shatter bonds and trigger even bigger rows in friendship groups. No one likes to be gossiped about at any age. But for adolescents who are acutely sensitive to what others think, it's particularly excruciating. Plus there's nowhere to escape to, if it feels like everyone at school is talking about you.

While gossip is an inevitable part of human interaction, it's still possible to help young people understand how it's used and thereby limit some of its damage.

HOW TO HELP

- **Ask them to check their motives:** If your child is spreading secrets or rumours, ask them to consider why. Is the target someone they are jealous of, or is gossiping part of their clique culture? Are they trying to win approval from their friends or do they not understand how hurtful rumours can be? Would they say the same thing if the subject walked into the room? Does it make them feel better to say something bad about someone else? Remind them we all exchange information about others as part of our social relations, but it crosses the line when it's untrue, unfounded, unproven or sets out to damage. Even if there's truth to the gossip, everyone makes mistakes. No one deserves to have private information made public for entertainment. Share your values about being fair and honest.

- **Talk through consequences:** Gossiping may be entertaining in the moment, but if your child is spreading malicious or false material, remind them that they will have to live with the constant fear it will get back to the person they are talking about. Like a balloon blowing in the wind, they can't predict where it will end up. Gossip won't buy friends either. While it might get the gossiper momentary attention, in the long term they are less likely to be trusted. Often, after the drama has passed, children who were seen to stir up trouble become disliked and rejected from the groups they were trying to impress. Remind them that the person they are gossiping to is also the person likely to be gossiping about them next time round.

- **Show children how to stand up to gossip:** Tell youngsters that something as simple as changing the subject is enough to send a message to the gossiper that they are not interested in taking part. If your child sees gossip on social media, they should exit the conversation. Other simple ways to pour cold water on rumour-mongering is for your child to respond with a positive statement about the person being talked about, like what they like about them. Without being confrontational, this alone is often a bracing reminder that not everyone is receptive to the story they are spreading. Get them to ask questions: Did the person telling the story see the incident? How do they know it's true?

■ **Rein in the reality celeb-spotting:** On a broader level, peering into the lives of celebrities has become a global hobby, thanks to gossip magazines and internet sites. Candid photos and snippets about famous people's lives trick us into feeling we know them, and have a right to take a view on their lives. Rein in your own judgement, so your child does not imitate you, and teach them that unless we are personally involved, we never have the full facts on which to base an informed opinion. Avoid school gate gossip too – your child will be watching you.

And if your child is being gossiped about...

When your child hears a rumour being spread about them, how they react will depend on how much basis it has in truth, how damaging it is and how ashamed and embarrassed they feel about it. Either way, reassure them that no one has the right to either compound a mistake by turning it into entertainment or use it to damage their reputation.

HOW TO HELP

■ **Stand up to it:** Suggest to your child that the best way for them to end any rumours swiftly is to go directly to the source, tell them what they have heard, how it makes them feel and say they don't want it spread any further. Even if there is some truth to it, suggest your child explains to the gossiper that it's up to them to decide what is said about their lives. Tell them they can neutralise its power by bringing it up first with their peers, addressing what's been said and giving their own truth. Help your child understand rumour-mongering by asking them what they think the gossipers have to gain by spreading it.

■ **Focus on the positive:** As a parent, offer your unconditional love. The rumour will be forgotten in time. Enable your child to find the time for friends who are loyal and who know them well enough to ignore untruths or exaggerations.

And even if it's not your child, help them tone down the 'drama'

'While I was talking to my friend about why she wanted to leave our group, we were both getting pretty upset. Then I saw another girl in our class film it on her phone so she could show everyone else. I have hated her ever since.'
Chloe, 12

Situations – like clique break-ups and rows – quickly escalate these days into what young people themselves refer to as 'drama' or 'beef'. This is amplified on social media and by other children on the sidelines, enjoying the spectacle as though it is a close-to-home version of a reality TV episode. Social media becomes their stage. Instagram is where the young people at the centre release their status updates on their feuds. Onlookers may also post Snapchat press conferences among their friends, giving their views on who's right and who's wrong in any on-going sagas. Help children understand that real people's lives are not soap operas and they don't have to join the supporting cast. When your child describes an unfolding drama, listen but remind them they always have a choice about whether to contribute. Often by getting involved, and taking sides, they will only get sucked in themselves – and when it's their turn to have the starring part, they won't enjoy the limelight.

Having best friends in primary school

'I have a lot of friends but my best friend is the one I have the most fun playing with and who "gets" me. It's still fun with other people when he's not around. Just not as much fun.'
Ben, 10

'My best friend and I are so close that we buy the same clothes, wear our hair the same and hope people will mistake us for twins. When we grow up we are going to buy a flat together and start a company.'
Lilly, 10

> *'Josh and his best mate are more or less drawn to each*
> *other like magnets. It's almost as if they see it as their*
> *natural way. They spark off each other like nothing*
> *I've ever seen.'*
> **Dinah, 37, mother-of-three**

At primary school, many parents worry about the fact that their child has not yet found their 'best friend'. Out of love and concern, we want them to have the protection of a 'special' companion who will be there to support them through the ups and downs of childhood.

Remembering our own school days, we may often wish they always have the security of someone to be with at break times and instantly have someone to go to with when the teacher says 'Get into pairs'.

Deep down, perhaps, we also feel reassured that our child is special enough to be chosen above all others, by another child. On the flip side, if they have not been picked by someone, we may feel it as rejection, almost as if they have been 'left on the shelf'.

So for all these reasons, best friendship has come to be idealised, not only in our own minds, but in our culture, film and literature, as a form of childhood 'true love'.

Yet it often helps for parents to adjust their expectations that every child should have a best friend. In the early years of primary, when it feels like all their other classmates are pairing off, this worry can lead youngsters to feel under pressure to go out and 'cast' the first person who's spare in that role, even when there is no natural chemistry.

Sometimes the title 'my best friend' is so sought after that a more dominant child can threaten to take the title away, if their playmate so much as plays with another. In the playground, the status of best friendship can be bartered by more controlling youngsters – as long as certain conditions are met. Yet throughout their school life, as long as your child is not lonely, and has someone to be with most of the time and is enjoying school, that's fine too.

If we over-egg the importance of a best friend, children can end up feeling like they are failing when, in fact, friendship comes in many different forms. Some friendships are intense, others are more relaxed. Some companions will stick around for a few weeks, others will last for years. The sum of all of these friendships add up to something positive in a young person's life.

HOW TO HELP

- **Understand your child's friendship temperament:** Some children are better suited to the intensity of one main friend, while others feel more comfortable with a wider circle. Some children actually don't want to be tied down – or don't feel that any single person can give them everything they need.

- **Encourage a wide social circle:** Even if your child has a good best friend, encourage them to play with others so the pair do not become socially exclusive or isolated.

- **Don't worry about rows:** Research has found that if your child has a best friend, this is the person they are the most likely to row with. But their close relationship also means they are more invested in making up afterwards. As far as possible, leave them to work out how to resolve disagreements.

THE BOTTOM LINE: *It's fine if children have a best friend – and it's fine if they don't.*

Best friends in secondary school

> 'I fell out with my old best friend. Now when I walk into a room, she walks out.'
> Lexi, 13

> 'My friend keeps sending me messages saying: "Do you love me? Tell me you still love me!". She's so insecure about our friendship. It's actually really annoying.'
> Amy, 11

A best friend, with whom your child can share everything, can be one of the best buffers against the stresses of adolescent life. Yet once again it's a relationship that can come with strings attached.

If these relationships become restrictive, controlling or one-way, they can throw up many more issues. A boy, who was initially happy that his best friend got the same trainers as him, may later become irritated when his mate buys the same sweatshirt.

A girl whose best friend nags her to only use the phone cover she gave her for her birthday, may get annoyed at the constant neediness.

HOW TO HELP

- **Look for other signs the friend wants to cool it:** Research has found there are three signs that a friend wants to end a friendship. The one who wants out of the relationship takes longer to reply to messages, stops returning invitations and tries to hint to the other they should spend more time with other people. Help your child to recognise when it's time to move on.

- **Help them get over the break-up:** While it's painful to see our children upset, they will inevitably encounter break-ups. How well your child gets over a split will depend on how mutually co-dependent they were, how bitter the fracture is, or whether your child has other friends to turn to. It will also depend on how much resilience and self-worth your child has developed. Don't underestimate the hurt and try to remain the calm voice of reason. Help keep your child busy and sociable.

If your child is too clingy

If you child is too clingy and puts others off by smothering, explain that this makes others feel uncomfortable and trapped – and will only make them want to get away.

In younger primary age children, this type of pressurising may be down to them not yet developing the understanding that others can have different ideas and desires from them.

They may believe that telling someone else they are their friend makes it a fact. Develop this by role-playing with toys to show what the other characters may be thinking when they are told they must play certain games, or can only play with one other toy.

With older children, talk through how it's also better if they give others space, rather than crowd them constantly, so friends really look forward to being with them.

Your child will be a little less possessive if they understand you can't demand friendship. It can only be given. Calling someone your best friend doesn't make it fact.

Helping children deal with peer pressure in secondary school

'One day I wore my hair in Princess Leia style space buns to school. By the end of the week everyone in my friendship group was coming into school with the same hair style. It was then I realised it was getting a bit out of control.'
Thalia, 12

'I got my son the latest soccer strip for his birthday but four months later he wants the new one because another boy in his group says his was out of date. He is so worried about not being "in" at school, I feel I have to buy it for him.'

Lara, mother-of-two, 38

There are times when Dawn wonders if her 13-year-old daughter Laura has completely taken leave of her senses. Last week, she snuck her older sister's brand new dress out of the house – without permission – in her school bag in order to pass it off as her own in front of her gang of friends. Dawn assumed she must have lost her mind because it wasn't exactly the perfect crime. Laura pictured herself on Instagram wearing it – but still tried for over an hour to deny it.

Then, despite the fact she and her friends were told off by another mother the week before for climbing onto the roof of the house where they were meeting up, once again the evidence turned up on social media. The group were snapped sitting with their feet dangling off the edge – with a 30ft drop below.

Laura is usually an engaging and charming child, and Dawn is at a loss about how to dial down the power of this magnetic pull on her normally sensible teenager. And as Laura gets older, she worries that if her daughter can't act sensibly now, what will it be like when she's at parties, where alcohol or drugs are on offer?

Young people are hugely dependent on their peers for their sense of well-being. We tend to think of peer pressure as something that exerts a magnetic power over our children during their adolescence. Yet, we may be more patient if we appreciate that it influences our actions all our lives. It is simply the basic human desire to belong.

In this case, Laura fell under its spell because she wanted to maintain her position as the 'stylish' one in her group and not be branded a wimp who wouldn't go out on the roof.

HOW TO HELP

For older children:

- **Meet your child's friends:** Teens are often afraid of letting you get too close to their friends in case you embarrass them. Even so, encourage your child to have their mates over, so they don't always have to meet somewhere where you won't have a clue what is going on. By offering to give your child and their friends a lift or to cook them a meal, you will also get to understand their friendships better.

How to help them stand up to pressure and say no when necessary...

- **Try 'What if?' questions:** You can help your child think about how to stand up to peer pressure, by playing a friendly game of 'What If'. Ask questions like: 'What if your friend dares you to play a drinking game?' Let them ask you questions too, so the game works both ways and they can hear how you would handle a difficult situation.

- **Suggest a repertoire of phrases to say no:** Saying no can take practice for anyone, but it gets easier over time – and when it's said at the right time with an assertive but non-aggressive tone, peers will respect those who can make their own decisions. Suggest children use phrases like: 'This isn't my kind of thing', 'Let's do something else instead', 'I'm not comfortable with that', or even just 'No, thanks', to make their boundaries clear.

- **Give them a get-out:** As your teen gets older, they are more likely to find themselves in sticky situations – like parties where they feel under pressure to drink or take drugs. Tell them if they ever find themselves in a scenario like this, they can always blame their 'annoying parents' or ring you to come and get them, no questions asked.

- **Keep talking:** Your child may fall in with a crowd that seems to have an obviously damaging influence. Even if your child defends their friends to the hilt, there will have been moments when they will have been put in an uncomfortable position and encouraged to act against their values. Even if met with eye-rolling or denial, explain your concerns. Deep down they probably understand your worry for their welfare. Lectures after the fact don't work. Children are more likely to listen when you are having one-on-one time with them, and you are not in conflict.

- **Get to know the other parents:** As far as teens are concerned, your ignorance about the parents of the other members of their gang is useful. It means they can operate their social lives without adult interference, and lie about their whereabouts because you can't check the truth of their story. From an early age, invite parents in when they come to pick up their kids, swap numbers and exchange texts so you form a united front, looking out for the welfare of all your children. If you know the other families, your children also won't be able to claim 'everyone else's parents allow them' – because you'll be able to ring them and check.

■ **Remain their biggest influence:** If we drive our children away with harsh judgement and criticism, it's no wonder they stop listening to us and move towards peers who don't yet have the life experience to know what's best for them. As they grow older, be accepting and invest the time to stay close, so that your family remains a group they want to belong to.

THE BOTTOM LINE: *Peer pressure can be positive as well as negative, and could help your child aim higher if they are friends with other youngsters who want to do well. However, in negative peer group situations, ask your child to check in with themselves with these questions: 'What am I being asked to do?', 'Why am I feeling uncomfortable?', 'Why do I have a feeling in the pit of my stomach that this is wrong?' They may not be able to dissuade their friends from their intended course of action (although they should try) but they can still stick to their own personal values.*

So when should you get involved?

A generation ago, parents mainly left children's friendship issues to them to sort out. Now parents are more likely to get involved. – firing off emails to other parents and demanding meetings with teachers and action from schools if we are not satisfied with the outcome.

But by sailing in to try to manage every situation, we deprive our children of the chance to work it out for themselves, make errors and learn how to handle conflict .

At the age of four or five, for example, it's relatively normal for children to say they don't want to play with each other if they don't feel like it. As long as the children are roughly equally matched – and it's not bullying – leave it to them to resolve disputes on their own. The truth is that even in normal playgrounds, little acts of social aggression come thick and fast between youngsters, and children have to get used to it.

In Japan, for example, pre-schoolers are expected to resolve their own conflicts – even if they resort to physical means, as long as no real harm is done. This attitude has been found to foster empathy and peace-making skills.

One of the toughest parts of parenting is to know when to step back and let your child suffer discomfort or emotional pain. But this is what we need to do if our children are to learn coping skills and be emotionally independent. In any case, children can't be forced to be nice to each other.

Furthermore, we may be bringing our own biases and childhood experiences into the situation, in which we mainly remember our worst-ever hurts, not the minor skirmishes that we survived. If we keep jumping in, we send a message to a child that they are weak and need us to protect them, when we should be fostering independence and teaching them the skills to handle flare-ups themselves.

So by all means listen sympathetically when your child says they have been hard done by. However, unless there's an imbalance of power between the two children or your child is being ganged up on or bullied, the majority of fall-outs are a chance to develop their conflict resolution skills.

How to help children navigate social media

'People think social media is all bad. But mostly I get support and compliments from my friends, like "cutee", "peng", "stunning" or "you slay my life". But there is a lot of pressure to get comments and get likes. Most people get between 80 to 90. If you're popular, you'll get between 100 and 200. That's when you know you are in the next league.'
Tamara, 13

'When my mum tells me to give my phone back, I ignore her because what's going on with my friends is more interesting. With social media, you're in charge, so it's a pain when adults start telling you what to do. I feel frustrated and isolated without it. But it does feel like the phone controls me, rather than the other way around.'
Harry, 13

'You see general comments about the type of outfit you've been wearing at school on social media later that day. You're pretty sure it's a reference to what you've been wearing, but you can't say anything. It creates massive insecurity.'
Chelsea, 16

'Of course it's not all negative out there. But anything that is bad out there gets amplified on social media. In a perfect world, I'd have the technology, without the rubbish that goes with it.'
Peter, 16

'When my son got bullied on an anonymous app, he was devastated. We tried to stop him seeing the remarks but he still wanted to know what was being said. It was like he needed to know so was prepared, no matter how much it hurt.'
Gabrielle, 48, mother-of-three

> 'A girl in my chat group commented about another girl, not in the group, that she felt sorry for her mother because her daughter was such a brat. One of the other boys showed the comment to his mother, who was a friend of the girl's mum. Next thing it gets back to the girl who is demanding to see my phone – and now there's a huge drama with adults involved too.'
>
> Leon, 13

For 15-year-old Nasma, bedtime is the prime time to flick through Instagram, Twitter, WhatsApp and Snapchat on her phone. She stays up until 1 a.m. around three times a week, even though she has school the next day. Once a week she keeps going until after 2 a.m.

Even if she feels ill with fatigue and eye strain in the darkness, Nasma still keeps going, for fear of missing out. 'There are times I have been looking at screens so much that my eyes have burned, I've got bad headaches and felt nauseous,' she explains. 'Now I sleep with my iPhone next to my pillow and put it on silent, so I can see it when it flashes.

'All my social networks are buzzing at 11 p.m. People will pose questions on Facebook such as: "Why do girls always flash their cleavage?" Then that turns into a row, with people piping up, tagging pictures of each other and saying "Do you mean her?". The more comments you make, the more you generate.'

For Luke, 13, the first thing he does when he opens his eyes is check all his social media. 'Sometimes overnight a big row has blown up. When that happens you just want to get the popcorn and a ringside seat because most of them are so classic. Some people will start off by posting, as their status updates, comments like "I hate so-and-so" and then it all kicks off. Most often it's girls throwing insults and making each other look stupid. It can be vicious out there.'

By the middle years of secondary school, many parents have almost given up trying to monitor their teens' screen time, assuming it was a battle lost long ago. Furthermore, a recent report from digital advice group Common Sense Media has found that half of teens now feel 'addicted' to their mobile devices.

However, as tech and social media researcher Danah Boyd has pointed out, young people are not so much addicted to phones, as addicted to each other and what others are saying about them.

After all, many adults find it hard not to check their own devices, so think how much harder it is for the youngsters afflicted by severe FOMO (Fear of Missing Out). It's not just that normal social cruelty is migrating to phones, It's also that such platforms invite impulsive responses, which are put in black and white. Others see the remarks, get drawn in and tensions quickly escalate.

It's not anti-technology or Luddite to point out that immature, reactive teenage brains mixed with social media can make for an explosive combination.

Yet when children ask for a phone as early as primary school, parents often agree, against their better judgement. Often they acquiesce because they want to be able to reach their child at any time for security reasons. If they don't, they also worry their children will be left out socially and won't be part of group conversations and social arrangements.

There is a balance to be struck. Young people who don't use smartphones or social media at all, are, indeed, at a slight social disadvantage compared to those who use them a bit. So there is a case for allowing them to have some access to social media.

However, from the start, most children lack the understanding of how addictive social media is and lack the life experience of self-discipline to impose their own limits. So, as a parent, you will have to explain how it's acting on them, and how to stay in control of it.

According to the latest research, the sweet spot appears to be allowing them to use social media for up to an hour a day. After that children's mental health starts to decline in proportion to how much time they spend on their phone.

Furthermore, the more time kids spend on social media, the more likely they are to lose friends. They are more likely to get into serious fights and be ostracised, participate in one-upmanship, empire-building or tiffs that drag on. A study by Israel's Hofstra University confirmed that the more time 14-year-olds were online the more likely they were to get caught up in cyber-bullying, with boys being just as likely to get sucked in as girls. Researchers found this behaviour peaks in Year 8 – and it's also worth remembering that British children spend more time online than any other nation. The price is high in other ways. The longer children spend on social media, the more likely they are to be depressed or lonely.

As parents, it's also time to take a more sober, objective view of how social networks have been developed to make the most of young people's social vulnerability and intense fear of being left out – and to be prepared to stand up to that.

It's now emerging that the designers of social networks and smartphones set out to make them addictive – and that they themselves know they are not safe for children. Many of the world's biggest technology gurus have now said they don't allow their own children to use the devices without strict parameters. One of Facebook's founders, Sean Parker, said the platform 'exploits a vulnerability in human psychology. God only knows what it's doing to our children's brains.' Before he died, Apple co-founder Steve Jobs told how he didn't allow his own children to use the iPad he had helped invent, saying he had strict limits on their technology.

Yet a third of pre-school children, age five and under, in the UK now have their own tablet. As Noël Janis-Norton points out in her book *Calmer, Happier, Easier Screentime*, while your child is an expert in knowing what they want in terms of phones and gadgets, you are always the expert in what's good for them.

From the outset, help your children understand that just like sweets, what they want in unlimited quantities is not necessarily healthy. Point out it's mainly the social media companies that benefit by adding features which encourage them to constantly keep checking their feeds. This is how they boost their traffic numbers and ad revenue.

Why else would Snapchat have developed 'streaks' – the rewards users get when they and another friend have sent each other messages for three days in a row? Any parent who has ever tried to prise a phone from a child's hand because they insist they must keep their streaks going, has seen for themselves how children are sucked in.

Phones are now a part of our lives and the way we communicate. Yet because they are still developing, children's overuse of phones is now being seen as a public health issue. And so it should, especially when research has found that the teenagers who spend five or more hours a day on electronic devices are 71 per cent more likely to have a risk factor for suicide. Young people who use phones too much are also 52 per cent more likely to have less than seven hours' sleep a night – with inevitable knock-on effects.

The result is that by the time they have left school, they may be sleeping one-and-a-half hours less a night than teenagers their age a decade ago. Beyond the physical toll, this kind of night-time phone use also makes young people more emotionally reactive and less able to control their responses – and for this reason, it's during these late night sessions that many issues flare up between peers.

Furthermore, when exhaustion strikes the next day, their nervous system feels frayed and they lose the ability to manage their rollercoaster emotions.

So if they have been up late on their phones, the upshot is children are more likely to be ruder to you – as well as more likely to fall out with their friends.

Stand firm. The bottom line is that a phone is not theirs if we are still paying the rental on it, as most parents are. Phones are on loan only, and there are conditions attached.

Support schools in their efforts to introduce limits. The majority of teachers now back banning mobile phones in schools completely, as France already has.

Some of the top schools in the UK now recommend children close down their social media accounts during exam periods. The more parents and educators work together, the easier it is for everyone to toe the line – and the less likely our children will be dragged into social media tiffs, under the bedcovers at 1 a.m. on school nights, which then causes their school work and their mood to suffer the next day.

As psychologist Dr Aric Sigman told me: 'I think we need to help children to ask questions of themselves so hopefully they can arrive at their own conclusions. And if not, we need to enlighten them. It should be one of the many health issues parents speak to children about, in the same way as they talk to them about nutrition, sex or puberty. Parents have got to sit down and say to their adolescents: "It's not that I don't want you on social networks. But most of your social life should be happening in the real world and the constant culture of comparison and bitchiness on these networks could also make you unhappy".'

Beyond that, Dr Sigman believes parents will find the resolve to place limits on kids' phone use if they start looking at the matter, 'not as a lifestyle choice, but as a straightforward medical issue'.

HOW TO HELP

■ **Set a limit on daily screen time:** Some children naturally seem to have a take-it-or-leave-it attitude to phones. Others can barely put them down, due to a mixture of temperament, FOMO and weaker impulse control. With these kids you will need to set limits, because you probably don't want screens sucking up most of the time that your child should be spending in the real world. At first this may feel like a daunting task, not least because you know your child is likely to become angry and even aggressive if they have had a free rein until now. To take the heat out of the conflict, and to help rules become routines, it may help to install a third party app which allows you to remotely set the times they can use their phones. When they know there is no budging, it shouldn't be too long before they learn to compress their social media use into these margins. Expect anger – as well as claims that 'no one else's parents' limits their child's phone use – but keep hold of the bigger picture.

- **Respect age ratings:** Parents may allow their children to lie and join social networks before the age of 13. But what sort of values are we demonstrating when we do so? To give an idea of what's at stake, cyber-bullying peaks at the age of around 12 – a year before children are even supposed to be old enough to be on social networks.

- **Keep an eye social on media use:** If the rest of the world is able to see your child's posts – and advertisers can track their movements to target them – it's not unreasonable for you to expect to be able to as well. Don't see it as waiting on the sidelines, ready to jump in the minute your child makes a mistake. Instead, view it as more about monitoring how your child is interacting with their friends and an opportunity to talk about what they should share and not share. Remember too that as they get older, phones may grant us **too much** access, which we would never have had pre-technology. As you get a sense of your children getting more mature, check who you're doing it for. Be careful not to let your own fears interfere with your child's opportunity to learn, and to exercise their own good judgement.

- **Reframe 'phone time':** Time without phones should not be seen as punishment. Instead, within your family, it should be seen as an opportunity to have more, not less fun, together. Let them pick a day out or a treat, in which everyone leaves their tech at home. By ring-fencing and planning gadget-free 'special time', you will also see your child's behaviour improve because they feel like they are the most important thing in your life.

- **Help them recognise how their phones make them feel:** As much as your child hates to be parted from their phone, they are probably already well aware that they don't always feel good when they are glued to them. They are likely to have already noticed how stressed and distracted they are made by the constant notifications, and how it feels when a friend seems more interested in looking at their screen than talking to them. Rather than nag, help them to recognise the physical symptoms of smartphone overuse too – whether it's eye strain, back pain, low mood or generally feeling overwhelmed.

- **Introduce phone-free zones:** Have phone-free zones around your home – for everyone. Just having a phone on the table has been found to get in the way of empathy, connection and conversation that your child needs to learn from you.

- **Introduce a digital sunset:** Place a limit of no phones or screens for at least an hour before bedtime. Make it a rule that all phones, including grown-ups', must be stored in a common area for charging. Any rule you set for them, should be followed by you too. Make getting enough sleep one of your family's priorities, and help kids recognise how it is linked to their emotional well-being.

What if you think your child is being bullied?

'My son kept hearing his two friends talking about another boy he didn't know. They said how annoying this person was and that he smelled. When my son, who was 11, asked who it was, they smirked. Then another boy told my son they were actually talking about him. He cried for days. I was lost for what to say.'
Karen, 36, mother-of-two

'When I was about 13, a group of boys at my school started bullying me on Facebook. There was no reason. They just seemed to hate me. It wasn't to my face. Instead they'd refer to me in the third person as a "him". They'd comment on photographs posted by my friends and suggest things like: "Why doesn't 'he' — meaning me — try out for the football team?" I didn't tell the school because I didn't think they'd do anything about it. In fact I didn't even tell my mum. I was too embarrassed to admit what was happening.'

Charlotte, 17

As we've seen, day-to-day social cruelty happens all the time in classrooms and children can be trained both to understand, and stand up to it, without any long-term damage.

Indeed, studies of playground behaviour have found that children in Year Six use behaviour that could be construed by adults as 'mean' around every three minutes. If we label everything as 'bullying', it says to children: 'You're not strong enough to deal with any unkindness on your own.'

Yet there are times when children do need help and those little flare-ups become more of a long-term flame.

'Normal' social meanness crosses the line into bullying when children are the target of ongoing, intentional campaigns of intimidation, by a peer who is more powerful than them – or ropes in others to join in with mean behaviour. But with the right support, most children can survive these episodes and feel stronger afterwards for having overcome them.

- **Step in:** If bullying is a problem already cropping up a lot for your child at primary school, intervene early. Take active steps to find out why your child is on the receiving end. A University of Warwick study found that children who are bullied at age six are significantly more likely still to be victims at the age of ten. Keep a watchful eye on their interactions with other children and why they might seem to be an easy target. Early intervention is important because entrenched bullying can cause high levels of isolation, distress and anxiety. Look for signs – which may include your child not wanting to go to school, passing bullying behaviour along to their siblings and or having difficulty focusing in class.

- **Stay calm:** However incensed you are, resist the temptation to go off the deep end in defence of your child. At this point, they need you as their firm anchor.

- **Take it seriously:** It's critical to support your child particularly if they are feeling victimised and worthless. Look though old family albums and remember the happy times. Tell them just because it feels bad for them now, doesn't mean it will feel like this forever. Help them be kind to themselves; encourage your child to do activities that help them feel better, whether it's exercise or a craft project. Reassure them you love them and it's not their fault. Encourage them to see friends they know out of school, who can remind them they are still liked and valued.

- **Don't let your child think 'Why me?':** Explain to your child that being bullied doesn't make them a wimp or a loser. Children target others for complex personal reasons, and sometimes because they feel threatened.

- **Help them work through how best to respond:** Whatever the reasons, other children will be emboldened to continue bullying behaviour if they believe yours is too scared to speak up. They are more likely to back off when your child takes a stand to name the behaviour, warns them they will tell an adult and so makes it clear they are not an easy target. Even if your child doesn't get the outcome they are hoping for, they have stepped out of their victim role. One way, recommended by educators and bullying counsellors, is help them practise saying straightaway: 'I don't like it when you say/do that. I want you to stop.'

- **Keep a record with your child:** If there is a longer-term bully-victim dynamic in place, empower your child by getting them to write down what happened, when it happened, and who was involved. If the bullying is online, keep the evidence – save or copy any photos, videos, texts, emails or posts. Screenshot any messages.

- **Go to the school:** If this doesn't work, then you will have to go to the school. As a parent, aim to deal with the situation as forensically and practically as possible to avoid further damage. Ask teachers to monitor the situation over time, because a socially powerful bully who has been caught out, may try and get back at the complainant by winning back sympathy via claims that your child got them 'into trouble'.

■ **Consider a new start:** Will it help your child to move to a new school? That depends on the nature of the bullying, the temperament of your child and how entrenched the problem is. Get an objective assessment from a teacher, or a pastoral care counsellor, who knows the peer group landscape of the school your child is at – and also of the school you are thinking of moving to. For some who are continually bullied, home-schooling can sometimes be the answer, especially now many communities have small local home-school groups and online learning is so much easier.

Lesbian, gay, bisexual and transsexual children

Bullying can affect any child, but children who are LGBT and don't fit into the narrow confines of how younger children think others should look, behave and act, can be particularly at risk.

This situation will probably get easier as schools and society as a whole takes a more relaxed approach to gender. But we are not yet there. Until then, there will still be some children who will take it upon themselves to be enforcers of what they perceive as gender 'norms'.

If you have a LGBT child, keep a special eye out and make a point of talking through their day. Form a strong team, and give them the validation and confidence of knowing that you are always on their side.

Set up a partnership with the school so they understand how your child wants to be addressed – and ask them to speak to the whole class, or better still the whole school, about LGBT young people.

Addressing other kids' confusion about the issue, and making clear the school has no tolerance for teasing or meanness based around that, is an important first step. Children often fear what they don't understand.

THE BOTTOM LINE: *There's never an easy answer to bullying. Some approaches will work. Others won't. But whatever happens, your child should be helped to make a stand to reclaim the power they feel has been taken away from them.*

And what if it's your child who's being mean?

'Last year, I was called into the school and told that my 10-year-old son had been bullying another child, along with a friend, and now that child was afraid to come to school. When he got home, I asked my son how he'd feel if someone did that to him. He cried himself to sleep that night, but then wrote the boy a letter to apologise. I think he genuinely hadn't realised how far he'd gone.'
Sam, 40, father-of-two

> 'A girl in my daughter's Year Four class wrote a letter which she pretended was from my daughter's best friend. It said she did not want to be friends with her any more and that she was annoying. The bully then folded it over so the real best friend did not see what it said and made up a reason to get her to write her name at the bottom. She then left it in my daughter's locker. My daughter was inconsolable when she read it. I can't think what would have made that child do something so premeditated and cruel.'
>
> Bea, 42, mother-of-two

Social scientists have now identified two types of children who show bullying behaviour – and they come from the opposite ends of the social hierarchy.

There are the popular children, who are often socially sophisticated and use such behaviour to grow their power and to make other children afraid to cross them. They may use bullying tactics, like exclusion and bitching, to turn others against someone they view as a threat. This kind of bullying is hard to spot, as these children generally already have the social sophistication to present well to adults – and hide what they are doing. The other kids who witness it are also unlikely to say anything, for fear of crossing the socially powerful child and putting themselves in the firing line.

The other type of bullying child has been identified as the 'bully-victim' – because at times they have been both. They fit the more traditional image of a bully and often belong to the neglected-rejected group we discussed earlier. They may have been targeted themselves by siblings at home, and the parents have not stepped in. They turn on others not so much to control, as to relieve their feelings of powerlessness and humiliation. Because they feel small, they manage their pain by making someone else feel smaller.

Often marginalised already, research shows these children also tend to be more impulsive and may show signs of other problems, like difficulties making friends. They often won't have a relationship with the person they target, but are more likely to choose a child who is exposed socially and has no one to stand up for them.

There is also a group of children who dally with bullying, at times when their own lives feel out of control. They seek to channel their anger by being aggressive and turning someone else into the punch bag, metaphorically or otherwise. Often this means behaviour may coincide with periods of upheaval at home, like the break-up of their parents' relationship, or a remarriage. Usually this behaviour will pass when they find their feet again.

Whatever is causing bullying behaviour, all these children need adult help, more than punishment, to understand their need to do this. However, in the moment – and whatever the cause – there are few more shattering situations than getting a phone call from school to say your child stands accused of bullying.

Our protective instincts mean that our initial reaction is to say: 'Not my child'. And it's true there is the possibility that another child is calling yours a bully because it's a way of 'bringing out the big guns'. If they were already mid-war, this could be another child's attempt to gain the upper hand.

Help teachers to find out if this is as one-sided as it looks. Is the other child really being persistently victimised by yours? Or is it two former friends falling out? Is it really that black and white? Both may have been the aggressor and victim. To get to the full picture, teachers will need to talk to bystanders and to other pupils who are not allied to either party, in order to understand.

However, if it turns out that your child is bringing others in to support them in victimising a weaker peer, has orchestrated a longer-term campaign against another child, or is using physical force and verbal intimidation on or offline, you will need to face up to what has happened and why.

HOW TO HELP

- **Listen to what's being said:** Few children will admit to bullying behaviour because they know how seriously grown-ups take it. Until you work out what has happened, tell your child to steer clear of their accuser and avoid doing or saying anything that will lead to more accusations. Instruct them not to try and rope in other friends to 'take sides' as that will justify the complaint. Tell the school you have spoken to your child and asked them to keep their distance until calm returns.

- **Help them acknowledge their part:** Depending on their age, personality type and emotional intelligence, some children will continue to insist it's everyone else's fault but their own, or claim the other person 'deserved it'. Even if they felt irritated or annoyed by someone else, explain that they always had the choice to walk away.

And if your child has been bullying...

You may need to take your relationship with your child back to basics and spend more time with them to find out why they felt the need to do this.

Their bullying may be a way of numbing and diverting them from their own discomfort. So, as a parent, it's important to reconnect with them in the ways I have described to try and address these painful feelings.

You may also need to do some serious soul-searching. For example, you may have to think about whether they've witnessed bullying behaviour in your own family, have been a victim of it, or are feeling lost because of upheaval at home.

Studies by the University of Norway have highlighted several factors in the home that can lead a child to bully:

- The parents are not involved enough in their child's life, and have lost their connection.

- The parents tolerate bullying behaviour, or don't set limits around their child's treatment of others. For example, these parents may take the view that 'boys will be boys' or think their daughter is showing leadership skills if she shows mean behaviour.

- When they discipline, parents may be overemotional or use force to discipline their child which the child then replicates outside the home.

Then there are the children who are less socially adept, and go too far because they have not developed the empathy to understand fully the effect their behaviour has on others. If you think that's the case, use the strategies in the last section on improving a child's emotional intelligence to help them foster understanding of how others feel.

- **Help them to practise empathy:** Ask them to role-play social situations – like imagining being a child who looks different, or seeing no one sticking up for a class-mate who is being bullied – so they can imagine different points of view.

- **Help them learn how to be a better friend:** Make more effort to notice and congratulate kind behaviour to help your child recognise when they are getting it right.

- **Ask them to take responsibility:** Your child can not learn unless they understand what they have done, recognise that others never deserve to be humiliated and understand the possible impact of their behaviour.

- **Allow them to move on:** Children need to know it's OK to make a mistake. Tell your child that you're confident that he or she can change their behaviour, because you know they are capable of kindness and empathy. Make it clear that because they showed bullying behaviour doesn't make them a bully for life. However, also make it clear that what they did was wrong, taking away privileges if appropriate, to enforce that message. Otherwise your child will feel it's acceptable to continue – even into adulthood.

Look at your family dynamic:

When you have more than one child, sibling rivalry is a fact of life. But when one child has more power over another and persistently uses it, it moves towards bullying. Bullying in the home is now being taken increasingly seriously as a precursor to bullying at school. The perpetrator either becomes used to being able to inflict it – and is not stopped. Or the victim gets used to playing this role – or passes it along outside the home. So forget any idea that when mean behaviour comes from a brother or sister, it's simply part of growing up and it doesn't do as much damage. After all, if you are a child who is suffering at the hands of a brother or sister, there really is no escape.

If, as a parent, you do nothing, you will also be a bystander. This will send the corrosive message to a child-victim that they are not worthy of protection and that this is their place in the world. If you realise that this is happening in your home, you will have to spend time with the aggressor to work out why they feel the need to do this. Do they feel the less favoured child and so they take it out on their sibling? Are they being bullied at school themselves and are looking for an easy target to take it out on? Do they have unresolved anger issues? You will also need to make amends to the child who has been on the receiving end.

Whether rivalry crosses into bullying or not, in every home, parents need to set ground rules that every member of the family treats others with basic respect. Values to include:

- You are not allowed to put down or humiliate your brother and sister

- It's not your job to point out your sibling's flaws (but compliments from a brother and sister can mean a lot)

- Don't destroy anything your sibling has made, harm any of their property or blame them for something you did

- Physical harm to a sibling is never allowed.

How to talk about bystanding

Even if your child is not being a bully, they may not realise they are contributing to bullying behaviour by standing by and saying nothing when they witness it. Talk about how this makes the victim feel afraid.

Talk about being an 'upstander'

At some time or other, every child is a 'bystander' who sees their peers doing something mean in a social situation. Bystanders say nothing when they see cruel behaviour, because they are relieved not to be the target. In other words, if it's someone else, at least it's not them. By contrast, an 'upstander' is someone who recognises when they are seeing something wrong and is willing to speak up about it, even if the person being teased or humiliated is not in their friendship group. By naming this sort of behaviour, and talking about how brave it is, you make it easier for your son or daughter to feel more comfortable about being one. Explain it doesn't take much to stand up. Just a few words, like: 'That's mean', 'That's enough' or 'Why are you saying this?' are often enough to signal to the aggressor they are losing peer support. As well as being an upstander, they can also be a supporter, who makes a point of backing up and going out of their way to be kind to a child who is being ostracised. Small gestures can make all the difference.

Social occasions

For younger children:

How to have happier play-dates

We tend to think that friendships just happen, as though they are down to chemistry. While it's true we can't force them, they can be helped along by giving children the opportunity to get to know each other. In their early years of school, giving kids plenty of practise can help them to build their social skills at a crucial age.

It's also important to build time into their schedules for play. In the increasingly pressured environment of today's more academically focused classrooms, children still need to have free time to connect.

Yet despite this basic requirement, a recent study found that overanxious parents are making children 'work' for more than fifty-four hours a week, even more than the average adult spends in the office. You are not doing 'nothing' by letting your kids have free time at home – rather than signing them up for after-school activities. As long as that time is not spent glued to screens or game consoles, see it instead as making a conscious decision to give your child time to find out more about themselves, and others, through their games.

Before a play-date, talk to your child about how to be a good host – and if there are any games they might like to play with their guest. If your child has any special toys they don't want to share, agree to put them away.

Once your guest arrives, be welcoming and interfere as little as you can in their activities. A study by psychologist John Gottman found that creative, imaginative play is the core feature of friendship – but it quickly stops if adults interrupt and burst that bubble.

And if a squabble does break out...

- Conflict helps refine children's social skills. So don't panic if there is an outbreak of tension. It has been found that the closer children are, the more they row. The tiffs are more quickly forgotten because they want to continue their game.

- If kids ask you to arbitrate, accept you will probably never get to the bottom of what happened. Ask them each to explain in their own words why they are unhappy. See if they can suggest their own solutions. Ask both to find their own middle way. If they were having fun, you will find that children are often motivated to come up with the answer to fix the tiff themselves. Give praise to each child for listening to each other and taking steps in the right direction.

- If kids still keep squabbling while playing the same game, suggest an alternative where they can play side by side. If there are enough materials to share, activities like drawing or crafts are less likely to lead to rows.

- When children have a friend to play with, research shows they have more fun and squabble less if most of it is outdoors. That's because there is less to argue over (after all there are unlimited branches, twigs and leaves). There's also more to explore. Children also bond more when they discover new things and have adventures together.

For older children:

How to have happier sleepovers

As kids grow, play-dates will turn into sleepovers. By the time your children are in the later stages of primary school, these will become the most hotly anticipated feature of many children's social lives.

Never hurry a sleepover with a child's new or potential friend, thinking it will make children closer. It's important that it's not parents who set them up but children, so let kids take the lead. Otherwise if your guest feels uncomfortable or homesick, it can be a bruising experience for all if they ask to go home.

As far as possible, keep sleepovers small, and limit them to well-established close friends. The more guests are invited, the more likely it is that someone will feel left out.

Despite the name, the last thing most children want to do is sleep on sleepovers, resulting in bad tempers the next day. So don't overdo them – and limit them as far as possible to holiday times.

Just because guests are coming should not mean your family values and boundaries fly out of the window. Beforehand, agree a mutually acceptable bedtime with your child – one that allows them to get some sleep but also feel they are staying up a little later than usual – and tell your child to relay your expectations to their guest.

If they feel embarrassed telling their friend that the sleepover will not be a free-for-all adult-free zone, tell them you can lay down the ground rules on their behalf when they arrive.

Your child may well say other parents let them do what they like when they go there, but that's rarely the case. Even if it is, explain that each family has its own set of rules and call their bluff by emailing or ringing.

Before the sleepover begins, warn your child that all phones and gadgets will be removed at an appointed time, and you will be keeping an eye on any social media posts. (Apart from anything else your guest's parents will not thank you if unsuitable pictures are posted – and they will partly blame you.)

Remember your goal is to be a parent, who is warm but also authoritative without being embarrassing. You want to create an atmosphere in which your child's friends feel at home, but also know there is an adult in charge.

Be welcoming. When they leave, thank them for coming and remark on one positive aspect of their behaviour so the sleepover finishes on an upbeat note.

How to have happier parties

'A vindictive mum in my child's class since nursery – and who has never liked me – deliberately left my daughter off the guest list for her daughter's first big party of secondary school. The girl was then primed to explain to my child when she saw her: "Oh, we don't talk much any more." It wasn't true – they still talked a lot – and other new kids she hardly even knew were invited. It was transparent that it was the mother's way of getting back at me through our children. I feel like saying: "You do know we're not the ones in Year 7, don't you?"'
Leah, 52, mother-of-three

'If I'm with a big group at a party, I'll turn on Snapmaps so everyone knows I am having a good time. It's a status thing – a way of saying: "Look what an amazing time I'm having". I don't do it to be mean. But I suppose other people will feel left out.'
Osh, 16

Lucy's party is set to be the event of the year. Her mother has arranged for her friends to hire out a local recording studio for two hours to make their own pop CD. That will be followed by pizza at a local restaurant. Of course some parents are thrilled to be on the guest list. Who wouldn't want such an exciting experience for their child? Others are less thrilled, even terrified, as it means they will to have raise the bar for their own child's birthday celebrations.

Then there are the parents whose children haven't made the final cut for the invite list – and are heartbroken because they know the event will be the talk of the class.

No longer the jelly and musical chair affairs they once were for primary age children, today's birthday parties have been transformed from personal expressions of love into public demonstrations of how incredibly special our child is – and so they have become far more talked about in classrooms.

As a parent it's important to keep them in perspective. If you look back on your own parties, you may recall the best moments were about the fun you had with your friends, not the venue or how much money your party cost.

HOW TO HELP

For younger children:

- **Take it down a degree:** Don't put pressure on yourself to make a party too lavish. Splashing cash on the event won't necessarily make it more fun for your child. In fact it can increase the stress on all sides. Make it more about what your child would love to do.

- **Consider inviting everyone in the class:** In the early years of school, consider inviting everyone. If you have a class of 24 kids don't invite 22 of them, even if your child insists there are two people they'd rather not have. As they get older, and parties get smaller, ask your child to be discreet about handing out invitations or send them by email or ask the teachers to put them in book bags so they are not opened at school. Will there be people who will be hurt by being left out? If they have friends who they think wouldn't fit in, because they don't mix well with the group being invited, ask your child to make a point of inviting them for a play-date or sleepover soon.

- **Don't assume it will be drama-free:** As they move up towards secondary school, some children may use the power they have over their guest list to reinforce the social pecking order. Talk beforehand about how being a good host involves making every single guest feel welcome, whether they are part of your child's in-crowd or not.

And if your child is not invited...

Put being left off the guest list into perspective. Although you might want to magically fix the problem by ringing the host parent and asking for an invite, it's better to help your child come to terms with the fact that no one's invited to everything. If your child is upset, share your own experiences to show it happens to everyone.

Even if you can wangle an invitation, by the time your child is eight or nine, they will know they didn't make the initial guest list. Word is likely to get back to the host child, who will gossip about it with the other children who are coming – and your child will look like a desperate wannabe. Furthermore, your child will be compromising his dignity, something that they should keep hold of in every relationship.

If you know your child will be unhappy having nothing to do while the event is happening, take their mind off it with a special activity you can do together and make them feel loved and valued.

For older children:

By the later stages of primary school, parties turn from fun events, mainly planned by parents, and designed to include as many others as possible, into more exclusive occasions, which will often be used to reinforce social groupings.

As the guest lists become more carefully honed, and these occasions become more important in their minds, this can also bring drama. In the early years of secondary school, the chatter around the anticipation and planning is almost as important as the party itself. On the day, your son or daughter will be eagerly looking forward to the opportunity to be undisputed leader of the pack for the night.

However, it's important to give them values so they use that social power carefully and don't use it to marginalise others or make themselves feel more important. Remind them that if they are old enough to have a more adult party in which they pick and choose the invitees, they are old enough to be diplomatic and thoughtful about its planning.

If your child is the host, ask them always to bear in mind what it's like to be on the 'Not Invited' list. Talk about ways to soothe hurt feelings by limiting talk of what will be happening at the party until after school. If another young person asks why they are not invited, suggest they have a thoughtful explanation ready.

Often if there's a question mark over whether to invite a particular guest, perhaps because they are going through some friendship ups and downs and your child is finding them annoying, suggest they invite them anyway.

If they are part of the larger peer group, and everyone else is invited, their visible absence will cause resentment and drama that could overshadow the celebration. Beforehand, explain to your child that it is a condition of your bankrolling of the event that they must be equally gracious hosts to everyone, not just those in their inner circle. That said, making sure the party is not too long, is well planned with no awkward gaps will usually give it enough momentum for no one to feel left out. Stay out of sight but be available. Often parties can throw up complicated social dilemmas and situations for young people. Promise to be discreet but say you are around if your child needs your help and advice.

Teach the skill of giving and accepting an apology

'One of my friends in my group posted a comment "Ur so ugly" on one of my Instagram posts. I was upset but said nothing at the time because I didn't want beef. When we had a row a few months later, I told her I was upset about it. She said I couldn't have been because I didn't say anything at the time. Trying to blame me for not wanting a big blow-up in the first place made me angry. If she'd just said sorry, it would have gone away. Now we hate each other and avoid each other at school.'
Caroline, 13

No one is perfect. Children need to know that there will be times when they take a wrong turn around the Friendship Maze. Saying the words 'I'm sorry' to someone they have wronged can wipe away some of the bitterness. It can be empowering for both your child and the person they are apologising to. By demonstrating and accepting humility, and showing empathy – a sincere sorry tells the person on the receiving end that the conflict is over – and the hurt is behind them. However, to have this effect, an apology needs to contain these components. The apologiser needs to:

- **Recognise they caused hurt and why**: A 'sorry' should not be delivered purely to get the apologiser off the hook or to manipulate the other person.

- **Acknowledge their responsibility**: 'People make mistakes' is not good enough. To say sorry, your child needs to accept they made a poor choice.

- **Avoid talking about what the other person said or did**: If your child blames or still believes the other person was 'being too sensitive' or 'took it the wrong way' they are not ready to apologise.

Tell your child not to be discouraged if they are not forgiven instantly. It can take time for others to get over hurt feelings or anger. Often the best that can be hoped for, is that it's a mature step that will help take some of tension out of a row. But showing your child how to take responsibility for their actions is a lifelong skill that will always help make them more decent people.

A word on reconciliation

> 'After a huge row with my best friend, she unblocked
> me on social media. That's how I knew it was all over.'
> **Sam, 13**

Children may go into rows, all guns blazing, but when the heat dies down, they regret how much the drama got out of control. Often after a few weeks, both parties have tired of the tension – and the constant stress they feel under – and wish they could go back to the way things were. At times like these, suggest your child just gives the former friend a genuine smile at school on the Monday morning after both have had a break. It may not work the first time, but it gives a clear sign that the conflict does not have to carry on – and often opens the door to relations getting back to normal.

Finally... how teachers can help

> 'The games teacher told us to get into pairs and I didn't
> have anyone to go with. It was the most humiliating
> moment of my life yet teachers do this all the time.
> Don't they realise how it feels?'
> **George, 11**

This is primarily a book written for parents. Yet teachers, who see more clearly than anyone how children interact, are the real power brokers who can change the experience of children in the social pressure cooker that is school. Every teacher knows that social cruelty seriously disrupts learning and that no child can achieve their potential if they are miserable and afraid of coming to school. Rivalries, divisions and meanness – and trying to cope with outbreaks of tension – make a teacher's job harder because classes in turmoil are harder to teach.

Yet looking out for relational aggression, rather than just overt bullying, and encouraging other pupils to stand up for ostracised students, has been found to reduce unpleasant behaviour like 'malicious gossip' by up to 72 per cent in classroom settings. It also dramatically improves children's school experiences.

Studies show that it's young people who have the greatest impact on each other's moral behaviour. But that moral structure still has to be taught – and that it helps when pupils are shown how to stand up for one another when they see unpleasantness, even if they find it entertaining, or they are just glad it's not them. It is teachers, not parents, who can harness the power of the most popular class members and identify children who are willing to use their social status positively, to stick up for victimised students.

By looking out for the different roles that children assume in the classroom, by allowing the pupils with the most social power not to hog top classroom positions and starring parts in plays, and by fostering a culture of teamwork in which pupils look out for each other, it is possible to disrupt the hierarchies that cause children to feel so trapped, and act against their better natures.

■ **Look outside the classroom:** The most socially sophisticated children may present a perfect face to you in the classroom. It's in the playground and at lunchtimes, that children demonstrate their clout among their peers. Researchers have found the most influential children will be the ones furthest away from the teacher on duty at break, so it's in these reaches of the playground where you may need to be most vigilant. As they get older, take a look around the lunch hall too. The same will apply there. The most socially powerful children will be the centre of their group, and be the first to get up from the table to signal they are ready to go.

■ **Check your own baggage:** Just as it is for parents, it is not easy to start from a neutral position when looking at children's social lives. When you are called upon to intervene in a social conflict, check if you have any underlying biases based on your own school experience. Where did you come in the social spectrum and is that influencing where your sympathies lie?

■ **Spot the patterns:** Just as parents benefit from understanding the roles children assume, so do teachers. Consider who in your class might fall into the popular, accepted, ambiguous, ignored and neglected categories – and how this might be affecting their behaviour and how they feel about school.

■ **Share out the jobs:** While not every child wants to be Queen Bee, they do want adults to be fair. Give every pupil a chance to have responsibilities and performance roles. Value different qualities in pupils other than being adult-pleasing and confident – or you are reinforcing social pecking orders, making more vulnerable children feel trapped by adult judgment too. Studies have found that one of the best ways to fade out social cruelty is not to reinforce hierarchies. The more students feel there are lots of ways to stand out and succeed, the better.

- **Take charge of social groupings:** Who doesn't remember wanting the earth to swallow them up, when they were the last to be picked for a team? When teachers allow youngsters to choose their seats and groupings, it can trigger unnecessary social anxiety, tears and humiliation. Studies have found that when teachers change around seating plans, or give children the chance to do non-competitive, non-academic activities where they can chat – like small crafting circles – the least popular children are more liked by the end of the year. Some schools have days when they mix up pupils so they have lunch together, and get to know others they wouldn't normally talk to. It will help to give young people active opportunities to get to know each other outside the pigeonholes they have put each other into.

- **Look out for meanness in PE lessons:** Meanness takes place everywhere in schools, but PE lessons are the easiest places for it to be hidden in plain sight. This is a lesson in which competition and physical force is not just permitted, it is encouraged. Indeed, one survey found that 77 per cent of the PE students said, as a result, that they did not tell their physical education teacher when they were bullied in these lessons. The rise in games like dodgeball, in which children get a chance to throw a ball as hard as possible at the legs of the opposing team, are easy opportunities for an aggressive, physically larger child to single out or intimidate another. Furthermore, sports skills are one of the qualities which can help elevate children to popularity. Reinforcing this by continually concentrating and praising a small group of athletically gifted youngsters reinforces social hierarchies.

- **Help children who are struggling socially:** It's probably already obvious who the rejected children are in your classroom. They consistently don't have friends and almost always end up sitting on their own. The longer it goes on, the more entrenched their isolation becomes – and if adults see what's happening and don't act, it can compound their misery – and they will continue on the same trajectory. Early intervention is important.

- **Intervene swiftly:** Teachers are privy to overhearing plenty of put-downs, gossiping and snide remarks in their classrooms. Yet one of the best ways to stop this behaviour is to act forensically, according to adolescent therapist, Signe Whitson, an established authority on bullying prevention. When you overhear something that disturbs you and seems intimidating, immediately get the child's attention, look them in the eye, and in a calm voice say: 'It's not OK to say that here. Do you understand?' The response must be direct, dignified and made crystal clear, without humiliation, that you take a zero tolerance approach in your classroom. As a role model, you will have set out the standards you expect and will also have won the respect of targeted children.

- **Identify and phase out bystanding:** Ultimately it's pupils, not adults, who have the best chance of preventing bullying – with your guidance. A study by Canada's York University found that when one child bullies another, 54 per cent of witnesses stand by and watch, 21 per cent imitate and only 25 per cent try to stop it. This makes the cruelty even more traumatising for the target, who assumes that everyone else agrees with what's happening. These bystanders are the same ones who will go along with directives to exclude and ignore the target child. However, if children are shown how to name this behaviour, and told that this is not an acceptable way to behave, they can learn to speak up for targets. They can be shown that standing up for others can be both 'cool' and the right thing to do.

- **Teach emotional intelligence:** It's understandable that in the highly pressurised atmosphere of today's classrooms, educators already feel they have enough to teach. But researchers have found that the benefits of emotional learning programmes last from six months to 18 years after – and that these pay off with improved standards. Encourage children to write their experiences and feelings down. This can help define problems in the students' own minds, and crystallise them more clearly for the adults in charge.

CONCLUSION

> 'My son used to be seen as the weird one in school. Now as he reaches the end of secondary, he's seen as cool. I think boys his age secretly admire the ones who don't feel the need to conform to everything. The key thing is to give your child the resilience to cope and the knowledge that school isn't forever.'
> **Jonathan, 50, father-of-three**

When you next welcome your child home after school, I hope this book will have helped you understand a little more about how their day has gone. Maybe you have new insight into why your son was late for registration because he had a couple of hairs out of place. Possibly it has shed light on why your daughter spends so much time hunched over her iPhone, waiting for the little 'like' hearts to pop up on her Instagram feed, showing that her friends approve of her recent post.

As a parent, it's difficult not to be affected by the hurt our children feel when they have friendship issues. Even in this hyper-competitive age, our concern has become so great that, for the first time, our worry about whether kids have healthy friendships has overtaken our concern about their marks.

How easy your child's friendships are depends on a combination of their biological temperament, what they have learnt from observing you, their life experience and their emotional and social processing skills. As you have seen, research shows that apart from innate personality, most of these qualities can be developed with support and practice. And even if you do have a more timid or impulsive child, empathetic parenting can still bring out the best in them.

Beyond that, I hope that by looking at how modern friendships have changed, how their social lives are organised and the phases your child will go through, you now have the perspective to stand back and be the calm centre for your child.

At times, this book has peered into some of the darker corners of what may seem like a juvenile game of Fortnite, played out over trivial details, such as the wrong kind of socks or or different skirt lengths.

Despite all this, 90 per cent of the time, our children work together, and practise kindness and consideration. When you look into the playground you will see most of them laughing and joking together. When they see their friends, their eyes light up. As they get older, their social group becomes the place where they feel they can truly be themselves, and their peers become the first people they turn to for comfort. With the right set of tools, there is no reason why many friendships cannot endure – or for any child to feel the need to turn into a bully.

By freeze-framing those odd moments of cruelty during the school day, children can develop the confidence to identify and deal with difficult situations. They can protect themselves so that social conflict leaves them with only light bruising which will fade with time, rather than serious body blows.

Though it may have seemed harsh at times to introduce the social bands that children fall into, this social science also helps us identify those most at risk – both at the top and bottom of the ladder.

The children who we see as mean and bullying deserve as much understanding as they do censure. There are always underlying reasons why children seek to control. Those with the most power need as much of our adult perspective as those with the least.

Now the next time your child hits a difficult social situation, I *hope* that instead of being tempted to put on your superhero cloak to try to rescue them, you will be able to give your child a thinking cap to help them work out what to do. By helping children recognise that conflict is an inevitable byproduct of human relationships, they will understand that it's nothing to be ashamed of.

When they understand they don't have to be popular to be socially successful, and that friendship comes in many shapes and styles, hopefully they will never feel like they have failed.

But there is work to do – and it starts with us.

We live in a world where we put a great deal of effort in helping children achieve, but not nearly as much time and energy is spent on making them decent. While we praise our children's academic progress to the stars, we don't celebrate moral development nearly as much.

We send them on enrichment and tutoring courses. Yet we rarely seek out experiences which will make them kinder, better people. We ignore these qualities even though the science shows us that being connected and empathetic is much more likely to bring them success and happiness in life. Indeed, the single best childhood predictor of whether your child will grow into a well-adjusted adult is not IQ, or exam results, but how they get on with other children.

Our best hope for the future is for us to be positive role models, putting away our phones to engage and prioritise our children, and demonstrating that all people deserve to be treated with dignity.

ACKNOWLEDGEMENTS

With many thanks to all of the following, as well as the many parents, children and young people who openly shared their experiences with me. Their names have been changed to protect privacy.

Noël Janis-Norton, Carly Silver, Christine Calland and Nicky Hutchinson of www.notjustbehaviour.co.uk, Janey Downshire, Julia Etherington, Michelle Garcia Winner, Anthony Harwood, Lily Harwood, Dr Aric Sigman, Caroline Montgomery, Anna Martin, Charlotte Stephenson, Amanda Goodhart. Plus a very special thank you to Clio Harwood.

FURTHER READING

Alexander, Penny and Goddard-Hill, Becky *Create Your Own Happy* (2018, HarperCollins)

Benson, Peter *Sparks: How Parents Can Ignite the Hidden Strengths of Teenagers* (2008, Jossey Bass)

Calland, Christine and Hutchinson, Nicky *Minnie and Max are OK!* (2017, Jessica Kingsley Publishers)

Carey, Tanith and Rudkin, Dr Angharad *What is my Child Thinking? Practical Child Psychology for Modern Parents* (2019, Dorling Kindersley)

Carey, Tanith *Girls Uninterrupted: How to Build Stronger Girls in a Challenging World* (2015, Icon)

Carey, Tanith *Taming the Tiger Parent: Putting your Child's Well-Being First in a Competitive World* (2014, Little, Brown)

Code, David *Kids Pick Up On Everything: How Parental Stress is Toxic to Kids* (2011, Createspace)

Damour, Lisa *Untangled: Guiding Teenage Girls through the Seven Transitions into Adulthood* (2016, Atlantic Books)

Downshire, Janey and Grew, Naella *Teenagers Translated: How to Raise Happy Teens* (2015, Random House)

Garcia Winner, Michelle *Thinking about YOU Thinking about Me* (2007, Think Social Publishing)

Garcia Winner, Michelle *You are a Social Detective* (2010, North River Press)

Gardner, Howard *Multiple Intelligences: The Theory in Practice* (1993, Basic Books)

Harari, Yuval Noah *Sapiens: A Brief History of Mankind* (2014, Vintage).

Honoré, Carl *Under Pressure: Putting the Child Back in Childhood* (2009, Orion)

James, Oliver *Love Bombing: Reset your Child's Emotional Thermostat* (2012, Karnac Books)

Janis-Norton, Noël *Calmer, Easier, Happier Parenting: The Revolutionary Programme That Transforms Family Life* (2012, Hodder & Stoughton)

Levine, Madeline *Teach Your Children Well: Why Values and Coping Skills Matter More than Grades, Trophies, or 'Fat Envelopes'* (2013, Harper Perennial)

Mosley, Jenny *101 Games for Social Skills* (2003, LDA)

Palmer, Sue *Toxic Childhood: How the Modern World is Damaging our Children and What we Can do About it* (2007, Orion)

Prinstein, Mitch *Popular: The Power of Likability in a Status-Obsessed World* (2017, Vermilion)

Semrud-Clikeman, Margaret *Social Competence in Children* (2017, Springer)

Simmons, Rachel *The Curse of the Good Girl: Raising Authentic Girls with Courage and Confidence* (2010, Penguin)

Simmons, Rachel *Odd Girl Out: The Hidden Culture of Aggression in Girls* (revised edition, 2011, Mariner Books)

Thompson, Michael and O'Neill Grace, Catherine *Best Friends, Worst Enemies: Understanding the Social Lives of Children* (2002, Ballantine).

Way, Niobe *Deep Secrets: Boys' Friendships and the Crisis of Connection* (2013, Harvard University Press)

Wiseman, Rosalind *Queen Bees and Wannabes: Helping your Daughter Survive Clique, Gossip, Boyfriends & the New Realities of Girl World* (2003, Piatkus)

Wiseman, Rosalind *Ringleaders & Sidekicks: How to Help Your Son Cope with Classroom Politics, Bullying, Girls and Growing Up* (2013, Piatkus)

NOTES AND REFERENCES

Introduction

Having friends is the single most important factor in making children feel good about themselves: Layard and Dunn *A Good Childhood: Searching for Values in a Competitive Age* (2009, Penguin)

Children spend more time connected: 'Children aged Five to 16 Spend an Average of Six and a Half Hours a Day in Front of a Screen Compared with Around Three Hours in 1995' *Childwise Survey* (2015) <http://www.bbc.co.uk/news/technology-32067158>

Screens can put a barrier between youngsters that reduces empathy: Uhls, Yalda 'Five Days at Outdoor Education Camp without Screens Improves Pre-teen Skills with Nonverbal Emotion Cues' *Computers in Human Behaviour* (2014) <https://www.sciencedirect.com/science/article/pii/S0747563214003227>

Bullying has been re-defined as repetitive, intentional abuse: UNESCO Definition of Bullying by Dr Dan Olweus, Professor of Psychology at the University of Bergen, Norway. Olweus, Dan *Bullying at School: What We Know and What We Can Do* (1993, Wiley-Blackwell)

Cruel words are as painful to victims as physical blows: Chen, Z., Williams, K. D., Fitness, J., Newton, N. C. 'When Hurt Will not Heal: Exploring the Capacity to Relive Social and Physical Pain', *Psychological Science* (August 2008) <https://www.ncbi.nlm.nih.gov/pubmed/18816286>

By four, some children have been found to be using relational aggression to make themselves more socially powerful: Nelson, D., Hart, C., Robinson C., 'Relational and Physical Aggression of Preschool-Age Children: Peer Status Linkages Across Informants', *Early Education and Development* (April 2005) <https://www.researchgate.net/publication/243962766_Relational_and_Physical_Aggression_of_Preschool-Age_Children_Peer_Status_Linkages_Across_Informants>

Sixty-nine per cent of girls between the ages of seven and 21 feel they 'are not good enough': *Girl Guiding Survey* (2016) <https://www.girlguiding.org.uk/globalassets/docs-and-resources/research-and-campaigns/girls-attitudes-survey-2016.pdf>

More than half of eight to eighteen-year-old boys would now consider changing their diet to improve their looks, and those who feel this way are more likely to feel depressed: Research by Media Smart (August 2016) <https://www.bbc.co.uk/news/education-37010205>

Field, Alison 'Prospective Associations of Concerns About Physique and the Development of Obesity, Binge Drinking, and Drug Use Among Adolescent Boys and Young Adult Men' *JAMA Pediatrics* (2014)

Children get less play: Gray, Peter 'The Decline of Play and the Rise of Psychopathology in Children and Adolescents' *American Journal of Play* (2011) <http://www.journalofplay.org/issues/3/4/article/decline-play-and-rise-psychopathology-children-and-adolescent>

Free play declined by at least a third between 1981 and 2003: Association for Psychological Science by University of Michigan <https://www.psychologytoday.com/blog/born-love/201005/shocker-empathy-dropped-40-in-college-students-2000>

UK schools are also cutting time spent on PE lessons because of exam pressures: 'One in three secondary school teachers said exam pressures were behind the decline, while 38 per cent said core subjects such as English and Maths had been given more time at the expense of PE' *Youth Sport Trust Survey* (2008) <https://www.telegraph.co.uk/news/2018/02/19/school-scrap-pe-time-exam-pressure/>

England's youngsters are the most likely, from within the 15 countries surveyed, to say that they had been left out by others in their class at least once in the last month: *The Good Childhood Report* (2015) <https://www.childrenssociety.org.uk/sites/default/files/TGC%20report_summary%20AW_Low%20Res.pdf>

Bullying is the fifth most common reason for school absence: Clery, Liz 'Estimating the Prevalence of Young People Absent from School due to Bullying' (2011) <http://natcen.ac.uk/our-research/research/estimating-the-prevalence-of-young-people-absent-from-school-due-to-bullying/>

Bullying is the most common reason parents choose home education: <http://www.calverteducation.com/should-i-homeschool/top-5-reasons-parents-homeschool-kids>

Children who seem to struggle to make friends may have problems decoding and interpreting the social cues they see other people using: Saarni, C. *The Development of Emotional Competence* (1999, Guilford Press). <https://www.guilford.com/books/The-Development-of-Emotional-Competence/Carolyn-Saarni/9781572304345/author>

Psychologists estimate that between 60 and 90 per cent of communication is down to facial expression: Mehrabian, Albert *Silent Messages: Implicit Communication of Emotions and Attitudes* (1981, Wadsworth Publishing)

Two of the most essential components – a sense of humour and good sharing skills – can be taught: Honig, Alice Sterling 'Humor Development in Young Children' *Research in Review* (1988) <https://www.researchgate.net/publication/234687359_RESEARCH_IN_REVIEW_Humor_Development_in_Young_Children>

When parents give their children good social coaching they have healthier relationships: 'Are They Listening? Parental Social Coaching and Parenting Emotional Climate Predict Adolescent Receptivity' *Journal of Research on Adolescence* (September 2015) <https://onlinelibrary.wiley.com/doi/pdf/10.1111/jora.12222>

Gregson, Kim 'Distinguishing Behavioral and Cognitive Dimensions of Parental Social Coaching: A Focused Examination of Parents' Social and Psychological Influence During Early Adolescence' A Dissertation (2015) <https://etd.auburn.edu/bitstream/handle/10415/4623/Gregson_Dissertation_AUETD.pdf;sequence=2>

One in 10 children has a diagnosable mental health disorder: *Young Minds Annual Report* (2015) <https://youngminds.org.uk/media/1233/youngminds-annual-report-15-16-final.pdf> <https://www.mentalhealth.org.uk/a-to-z/c/children-and-young-people>

PART ONE – WHAT'S CHANGED IN OUR CHILDREN'S FRIENDSHIPS

Our schools have become bigger, more crowded and more impersonal: Lightfoot, Liz 'Supersize Schools: How Big is too Big... 2,000? Or 4,000?' *The Guardian* (October 2015) <https://www.theguardian.com/education/2015/oct/27/supersize-schools-too-big-add-places-pupils>

Abrams, Fran 'The Growth of Titan Schools' *The Guardian* (23 April 2012) <https://www.theguardian.com/education/2012/apr/23/titan-schools-primary-largest-school-population>

The Programme for International Student Assessment (PISA) is a worldwide study by the Organisation for Economic Co-operation and Development (OECD) in member and non-member nations intended to evaluate educational systems by measuring 15-year-old school pupils' scholastic performance on mathematics, science, and reading. It began in 2000 and has been repeated every three years with the aim of helping nations improve their data and help these countries to improve their education polices and results

Competition – and how it's changed childhood

Competition in classrooms raised by a competitive school system, and government pressure for better results and higher placings in international PISA results: 'Government wanted UK schools to be among best in OECD's Pisa assessment, but Scotland and Wales rankings have fallen' *The Guardian* (December 2016) <https://www.theguardian.com/education/2016/dec/06/english-schools-core-subject-test-results-international-oecd-pisa>

Gove, Michael 'PISA Slip Should put a Rocket Under our World-class Ambitions and Drive us to Win the Education Space Race' the *Times Educational Supplement* (17 December 2010)

Competition can seep into children's relationships early: Harris, Malcolm 'Competition Is Ruining Childhood. The Kids Should Fight Back' *New York Times* (6 November 2017) <https://www.nytimes.com/2017/11/06/opinion/students-competition-unions-bargaining.html>

Teenage girls who feel they have to compete and conform in a competitive world can become hyper-vigilant to threat: Hamilton, Maggie *What's Happening to our Girls?* (Viking, 2009) <https://www.youtube.com/watch?v=6T8QIiU09pc>

Kids who are raised with a cooperative approach to their peers are likely to be more emotionally resilient, creative and open-minded: Kohn, Alfie *No Contest: The Case Against Competition* (2002, Houghton Mifflin)

Whitebread, Dr D., Basilio, M, Kuvalja, M., and Verma, M., 'The Importance of Play: A Report on the Value of Children's Play with a Series of Policy Recommendations' *University of Cambridge* (2012) <http://www.csap.cam.ac.uk/media/uploads/files/1/david-whitebread---importance-of-play-report.pdf>

Why there's no minimum age on meanness

Aggression starts sooner, as early as the age of four: Nelson, D., Hart, C., Robinson, C., 'Relational and Physical Aggression of Preschool-Age Children: Peer Status Linkages Across Informants' *Early Education and Development* (April 2005)

Boys are using the same methods just as much by the end of primary school: Survey by MediaSmarts of 5,436 students in Year Four to 11 (March 2014)

Relational aggression among boys: Eiksen, Ingunn Marie 'Blind Spots and Hidden Dramas' *Gender and Education* (August 2016)

Sticks and stones and sugar and spice: Owens, LD 'Girls' and Boys' Aggression in Schools' *Australian Journal of Guidance and Counselling* (1996)

A third of pre-school children have a tablet: *Childwise Report* (2017) <http://www.dailymail.co.uk/health/article-4968176/A-British-children-five-tablets.html>

Growing older younger – how physically growing up too soon also affects friendships

Children are reaching puberty five years earlier than a century ago: Biro, F. M. et al 'Onset of Breast Development in a Longitudinal Cohort' *Pediatrics* (December 2013) <https://www.ncbi.nlm.nih.gov/pubmed/24190685>

Journal of Epidemiology and Community Health: Trends in Menarchal Age: Özen, S. and Darkan, S., *'Effects of Environmental Endocrine Disruptors on Pubertal Development'* (2011). Why children are going through puberty earlier: Pinkney, J., Streeter, A., Hosking, J., Mohammod, M., Jeffery, A., Wilkin, T., 'Adiposity, Chronic Inflammation, and the Prepubertal Decline of Sex Hormone Binding Globulin in Children: Evidence for Associations With the Timing of Puberty' *The Journal of Clinical Endocrinology & Metabolism* <https://academic.oup.com/jcem/article/99/9/3224/2538136>

White boys are starting to mature at ten and black boys at nine: *American Academy of Paediatrics* (October 2012) <http://pediatrics. aappublications.org/content/pediatrics/early/2012/10/15/peds.2011- 3291.full.pdf>

Carey, Tanith Interview with Nigel Latta from 'The Little Boys Going Through Puberty at Nine' the *Daily Mail* (13 February 2003). <https:// www.dailymail.co.uk/femail/article-2274678/We-know-girls-reaching- sexual-maturity-sooner-But-theres-equally-disturbing-trend-parent- ignore-The-little-boys-going-puberty-NINE.html>

How the rise of reality TV impacts children's social relationships

More than 1,000 studies have drawn a link between TV violence and aggressive behaviour in children: Huesmann, L. R., Moise-Titus, J., Podolski, C., & Eron, L. D. 'Early Exposure to TV Violence Predicts Aggression in Adulthood' *Developmental Psychology* (2003) <http://www. apa.org/pi/prevent-violence/resources/tv-violence.aspx>

Girls who regularly watch reality TV accept and expect more aggression in their lives: <https://www.girlscouts.org/content/dam/ girlscouts-gsusa/forms-and-documents/about-girl-scouts/research/ real_to_me_factsheet.pdf>

Cruel intentions on television and in real life: Coyne, S. M., Archer, J. and Eslea, M., 'Can Viewing Indirect Aggression Increase Viewers' Subsequent Indirect Aggression?' *Journal Of Experimental Child Psychology* (2004)

Coyne, S. M., Archer, J. and Eslea, M.,' "We're not friends any more! unless..." The Frequency and Harmfulness of Indirect, Relational, and Social Aggression.' *Aggressive Behavior* (2006)

'Just "harmless entertainment"? Effects of Surveillance Reality TV on Physical Aggression' <http://psycnet.apa.org/record/2014-33476-001>

As a result girls age 15, find conflict entertaining, and spreading nasty stories was something to do to create excitement in their lives: 'Soap Opera Spite Turns School Beauties into Beasts' *The Sun Herald* (24 March 2002)

Reality TV shows contain an average of 85 verbal attacks, insults and snide remarks each hour – almost twice that of comedies, dramas and soap operas: Coyne, S. M., Robinson S. L. and Nelson D. A. 'Does Reality Backbite? Physical, Verbal, and Relational Aggression in Reality Television Programs' *Journal of Broadcasting & Electronic Media* (2010) <https://doi.org/10.1080/08838151003737931>

How being busy affects our children's social skills

Adults are spending less time talking to kids: 'Do you Spend More Time With your Phone than your Family? Parents and Children Exchange 5,800 Texts and 260 Emails a Year' the *Daily Mail* (April 2016) <http://www.dailymail.co.uk/sciencetech/article-3550241/Do-spend-time-phone-family-Parents-children-exchange-5-800-texts-260-emails-year.html>

Half of parents routinely allow infants to play with their iPhone or tablet. One in seven allow their tot to spend more than four hours a day playing with their gadget: *Babies.co.uk* <https://www.mirror.co.uk/news/uk-news/tablets-ipad-used-parents-calm-2332807>

The other outcome is that some youngsters start school without the skills to make friends: *Midwives Magazine* (December 2004) <https://www.rcm.org.uk/news-views-and-analysis/analysis/talk-to-your-baby>

Ashiabi, G. S. 'Play in the preschool classroom: Its socio-emotional significance and the teacher's role in play' *Early Childhood Education Journal, 35*, 199-207 (2007)

Make-believe play versus academic skills: Bodrova, Vygotskian, E. A., 'Approach to Today's Dilemma of Early Childhood Education' *European Early Childhood Education Research Journal* (2008)

Around the world, many experts now recommend that under twos get no screen time, except for face time: American Pediatric Association, Canadian Paediatric Society <https://www.aap.org/en-us/about-the-aap/aap-press-room/Pages/American-Academy-of-Pediatrics-Announces-New-Recommendations-for-Childrens-Media-Use.aspx>

These days the nursery 'curriculum' is far less free and easy: Early Years Foundation Stage <https://www.gov.uk/early-years-foundation-stage>

Youngsters who have healthy relationships with the adults in their lives are more likely to have healthy peer friendships: Lee, R. K., Roisman, G. I., Fraley, R. C., Simpson, J. A., 'The Enduring Predictive Significance of Early Maternal Sensitivity: Social and Academic Competence Through Age 32 Years' (December 2014).<https://doi.org/10.1111/cdev.12325>

Head teachers are continuing to cut break-times and playtimes to keep up with curriculum requirements: A report from the Nuffield Foundation found that schools have been cutting break time since 2006. <https://www.nuffieldfoundation.org/sites/default/files/Breaktimes_Final%20report_Blatchford.pdf>

Press Association 'Children Starting School Unable to Speak or use Toilet, Ofsted Head Warns' *The Telegraph* (1 June 2018) <https://www.telegraph.co.uk/news/2018/06/01/children-starting-school-unable-speak-use-toilet-ofsted-head/>

Turner, Camilla 'Parents Sending Children to School Unable to Speak Properly, says Education Secretary' *The Telegraph* (31 July2018) <https://www.telegraph.co.uk/education/2018/07/30/parents-sending-children-school-unable-speak-properly-says-education/>

Hunt blames smartphone for children not speaking properly: Morton, Katy *Nursery World* (August 2015) <https://www.nurseryworld.co.uk/nursery-world/news/1153010/hunt-blames-smartphones-for-children-not-speaking-properly>

It takes 391 separate communication processes for a three-year-old to respond to the question: 'Not on Speaking Terms: Why do many Children Lack Basic Language Skills?' asks Anne-Marie Sapsted, *The Daily Telegraph* (3 April 2004)

'I Can' Report which found that almost all nursery staff have one child in the nursery with communication problems. Ten per cent said they had 10 or more children with difficulties (February 2004)

As one education minister put it, you don't want toddlers 'running around with no sense of purpose': Williams, Martin 'Childcare Minister Elizabeth Truss Attacks Unruly Nurseries' interview *The Guardian* (22 April 2013) <https://www.theguardian.com/education/2013/apr/22/childcare-minister-elizabeth-truss-nurseries>

Children's requirement for happiness: 'Child Wellbeing in Rich Countries: A Comparative Overview' (2013) <https://www.unicef-irc.org/publications/pdf/rc11_eng.pdf>

Among children aged two to five, 69 per cent can open a web page browser, yet only 20 per cent know how to swim: *Play England Report* (2008) <http://www.dailymail.co.uk/news/article-1040447/Cotton-wool-parenting-holding-children-says-study.html>

How getting on with other parents helps your child's friendships

'A school that has a problem with cliques among students often have problems with cliques among the parents as well': Thompson, Dr Michael *Mom, They're Teasing Me: Helping Your Child Solve Social Problems* (Ballantine Books December 2008)

How social media has changed friendship

'Help them keep a sense of proportion.': Quotes from Robert Faris, Associate Professor of Sociology at the University of California. CNN SPECIAL REPORTS 'Being 13: Inside the Secret World of Teens' (1 December 2015) <http://transcripts.cnn.com/TRANSCRIPTS/1512/01/csr.01.html>

Who climbs the highest on the social ladder?

Experiments have revealed how just putting people in the same shirt or telling them they have the same tastes (even when they don't) can make them clump together and feel hostile against other groups who are even the slightest bit different: Smucker, B., Creekmore, A. M., 'Adolescents' Clothing Conformity, Awareness, and Peer Acceptance' (December 1972) <https://doi.org/10.1177/1077727X7200100203>

Social scientists have also found that a pecking order forms: Pattiselanno, K., Dijkstra, J. K., Steglich, C., Vollebergh, W., Veenstra, R., 'Structure Matters: The Role of Clique Hierarchy in the Relationship Between Adolescent Social Status and Aggression and Prosociality' *Journal of Youth and Adolescence* (2015) <https://www.ncbi.nlm.nih.gov/pubmed/26077559> <https://www.ncbi.nlm.nih.gov/pmc/articles/PMC4636991/>

Human brains are hard-wired to seek status. Scans have found the brain circuitry associated with this desire to be top dog: National Institute of Mental Health of the National Institutes of Health, Bethesda, Maryland. Zink, C., Tong, Y., Chen, Q., Bassett, D., Stein, J., Meyer-Lindenberg, A., 'Know Your Place: Neural Processing of Social Hierarchy in Humans' *Neuron* (April 2008) <https://www.ncbi.nlm.nih.gov/pmc/articles/PMC2430590/>

Their brains have also been found to derive more pleasure from social acceptance than adult brains do: Albert, D., Chein, J., Steinberg, L., 'The Teenage Brain' (April 2013) <https://www.edweek.org/ew/articles/2013/05/22/32peers.h32.html>

Cliques start to become more clearly defined in Year Four: Boderick, P. C., Blewitt, P., Bacon, P. A., 'Why Do Cliques Form?' (2010, Prentice Hall) <https://www.education.com/reference/article/why-do-cliques-form/>

McFarland, Daniel A., Professor of Education at Stanford Graduate School of Education *American Sociological Review* <http://www.dailymail.co.uk/sciencetech/article-2829445/The-end-mean-girls-Researchers-cliques-form-high-school-say-know-end-them.html>

Boys' and girls' self-esteem falls off a cliff between the age of about 13 and 15: Robins, R. W., Trzesniewski, K. H., 'Self-Esteem Development Across the Lifespan' *Current Directions in Psychological Science,* Department of Psychology, University of California, Davis, and Institute of Psychiatry, King's College, London (2015) <http://www.psy.miami.edu/faculty/dmessinger/c_c/rsrcs/rdgs/emot/robins_trz.selfesteemdevel_curidr2005.pdf>

Unselfish people are happier than people who are preoccupied with their own position: Dunn, Judy and Layard, Richard, *A Good Childhood: Searching for Values in a Competitive Age* (Penguin, February 2009)

There are four main types of parenting: authoritative, neglectful, permissive, and authoritarian (December 2013) <https://my.vanderbilt. edu/developmentalpsychologyblog/2013/12/types-of-parenting-styles-and-how-to-identify-yours/>

PART TWO – HOW TO UNDERSTAND YOUR CHILD'S SOCIAL LIFE

How Classrooms Break Down into Bands

Social science studies have found consistently the same breakdowns of popular and unpopular class in every group they test: How classrooms break down into bands: Accepted, Controversial, Neglected, Rejected: Newcomb, A. F., Bukowski, W. M., and Pattee, L., 'Children's Peer Relations: A Meta-analytic Review of Popular, Rejected, Neglected, Controversial, and Average Sociometric Status', *Psychological Bulletin, 113, 99-128* (1993) <https://www.ncbi.nlm.nih.gov/pubmed/8426876>

There are two types of popularity: Prinstein, Mitch *Popular: The Power of Likability in a Status-Obsessed World* (2017, Vermillion)

It takes just a small number of good friends for children to be happy: Layard, Richard and Dunn, Judy, *A Good Childhood: Searching for Values in a Competitive Age* (2009, Penguin)

Any class is a drama that requires different characters. The hierarchy and the roles are 'assigned': Thompson, Michael *Mom, They're Teasing Me: Helping Your Child Solve Social Problems* (2008, Ballantine Books)

How Friendship Grows and Changes Through Childhood

Children can also already understand other people's emotions and why they feel them: *Is Empathy Learned – or Are We Born with It?* (December 2, 2012) <http://www.developmentalscience.com/blog/2012/12/02/is-empathy-learned-or-are-we-born-with-it>

Children are drawn to peers with the same level of play, social skills and assertiveness: 'Future Directions in... Friendship in Childhood and Early Adolescence' *Social Development* (November 2008) <https://www.ncbi.nlm.nih.gov/pmc/articles/PMC5619663/>

Aboud, F. E., Mendelson, M. J. *Determinants of Friendship Selection and Quality: Developmental Perspectives*

Bukowski, William M. *The Company they Keep: Friendship in Childhood and Adolescence* (1996, Cambridge University Press)

According to anthropologist Desmond Morris, rows at this age break out for three reasons: Morris, Desmond *Child* (2010, Hamlyn)

When asked to make a decision, children this age will go with the majority: Killen, M., Rutland, A., Abrams, D., Mulvey, K. L., Hitti, A. 'Development of Intra- and Intergroup Judgments in the Context of Moral and Social-Conventional Norms' *Child Development* (November 2012) <https://onlinelibrary.wiley.com/doi/abs/10.1111/cdev.12011>

Girls now tend to form smaller friendship groups and are tending to form bigger gangs and play over wider areas: Edwards, C. P., Knoche, L., Kumru, A., 'Play Patterns and Gender'. University of Nebraska, Lincoln (2001) <https://digitalcommons.unl.edu/cgi/viewcontent.cgi?article=1610&context=psychfacpub>

As long as children are smiling and laughing during play-fighting, serious injuries are rare: Carlson, Frances M. 'Rough Play – One of the Most Challenging Behaviours' National Association for the Education of Young Children <https://guidingchildrensbehaviorkaceys.weebly.com/uploads/2/3/2/7/23273454/roughplay.pdf>

Who's Who in Girls' Cliques?

Each member has their own role in the hierarchy which naturally forms: Wiseman, Rosalind *Queen Bees and Wannabes: Helping your Daughter Survive Cliques, Gossip, Boyfriends and the Realities of Girl World* (2003, Piatkus)

Wiseman, Rosalind *Ringleaders and Sidekicks: How to Help Your Son Cope with Classroom Politics, Bullying, Girls and Growing up* (2013, Piatkus)

How Boys' and Girls' Friendships are Different

Boys generally play in more physically active ways – and even the more energetic girls don't have the same drive to run around: Telford, R. M., Telford, R. D., Olive, L. S., Cochrane, T., Davey, R., 'Why Are Girls Less Physically Active than Boys? Findings from the LOOK Longitudinal Study' *PLOS ONE* (March 2016) <https://journals.plos.org/plosone/article/comments?id=10.1371/journal.pone.0150041>

Boys' and Girls' Brains are Different: Gender Differences in Language Appear Biological: Burmann, D. D., Bitan, T., Booth, J. R., 'Sex Differences in Neural Processing of Language Among Children' *Neuropsychologia* (2008) <https://www.ncbi.nlm.nih.gov/pubmed/18262207>

https://www.ncbi.nlm.nih.gov/pubmed/18262207 Some of these differences in play preferences seem to be partly down to the influence of male hormones – on boy babies' brains in the womb: Hines, M.,

Constantinescu, M., Spencer, D., 'Early Androgen Exposure and Human Gender Development' *Biology of Sex Differences* (2015) <https://bsd. biomedcentral.com/articles/10.1186/s13293-015-0022-1>

While girls use words to build rapport, boys use them to build status: Tannen, Deborah *You Just Don't Understand: Women and Men in Conversation* (2013, William Morrow)

How to Tackle Boys' Friendship Problems

Parent often unknowingly perpetuate the belief that boys should hide their hurt: Kindlon, Dan and Michael Thompson *Raising Cain: Protecting the Emotional Life of Boys* (2000, Ballantine)

Boys must be allowed to express their feelings just as freely: Pollack, William *Real Boys: Rescuing Our Sons from the Myths of Boyhood* (1999, Henry Holt & Company)

Mothers are more likely to use emotional words when talking to their four-year-old daughters: Aznar, A., Tenenbaum, H. R., 'Gender and Age Differences in Parent-child Emotion Talk' *The British Journal of Psychology* (November 2014)

Yoder, Janice D. *Women and Gender: Transforming Psychology* (2002, Pearson)

Growing UP: Learning to be Ourselves in a Gender-Polarized World <https://j. b5z.net/i/u/2084689/f/yod_ch04.pdf>

Decide on your Values

Parents and children should come up with a 'family mission statement' to create a vision of what you are about: Covey, Stephen R. *7 Habits of Highly Effective Families* (1999, Simon & Schuster)

Teaching your child to be kind also brings long term health benefits: <https://greatergood.berkeley.edu/article/item/kindness_makes_you_happy_and_happiness_makes_you_kind>

Studies have found that youngsters who have healthy relationships with the adults in their lives are more likely to have healthy peer friendships: James, Alana 'How your Childhood Experiences Shape your Social Skills as an Adult' the *Independent* (3 March 2016)

Birth order can be factor in how children relate to friends: Shuitemaker, Lisette and Enthoven, Wies, *The Eldest Daughter Effect – How First Born Women – like Oprah Winfrey, Sheryl Sandberg, J. K. Rowling and Beyoncé – Harness their Strength* (2016, Findhorn Press)

The hearts of the shyer children beat consistently faster than other babies: Reznick, J. S., Kagan, J., Snidman, N., Gersten, M., Baak, K., Rosenberg, A., 'Inhibited and Uninhibited Children: A Follow-Up Study' *Child Development Vol. 57, No. 3 pp. 660-680* (June 1986) <https://www.jstor.org/stable/1130344?seq=1#page_scan_tab_contents>

'Emotion is every bit as much a function of the brain as intelligence': Elliott, Lise *Early Intelligence: How the Brain and Mind Develop in the First Five Years of Life* (2001, Penguin)

PART THREE – HOW TO HELP YOUR CHILD MAKE AND KEEP FRIENDS

While it takes the average youngster less than a second to read social cuesfor some youngsters it can take a little longer: Carey, Tanith: Michelle Garcia Winner interview: 'Does your Child Struggle to Make Friends? They Could be Suffering From Social Dyslexia' *Daily Telegraph* (31 August, 2016) <https://www.telegraph.co.uk/family/parenting/does-your-child-struggle-to-make-friends-they-could-be-suffering/>

Roughly 10 per cent of children have problems understanding non-verbal signals: Nowicki Jr, Dr. Stephen and Duke, Dr. Marshall P. *Helping the Child Who Doesn't Fit In* (Peachtree Publishers, 1992)

'Helping Children Overcome Rejection', *New York Times* <https://www.nytimes.com/1992/08/19/health/personal-health-922392.html>

Carey, Tanith 'Unpopular Kids: Why Don't They Like Me?' The Independent (15 February 2011) <https://www.independent.co.uk/life-style/health-and-families/features/unpopular-children-why-dont-they-like-me-2214956.html>

How to help improve your child's social skills

Semrud-Clikeman, Margaret *Social Competence in Children* (Springer, 2007) <https://www.springer.com/gb/book/9780387713656>

Experts who analysed the eating habits of more than 24,000 children, aged six to 11, found they had better social skills if they regularly sat around the table with their families: Lora K. R., Sisson S. B., DeGrace B. W., 'Frequency of Family Meals and 6–11-year-old Children's Social Behaviours', Morris *Journal of Family Psychology* (August 2014) <https://www.ncbi.nlm.nih.gov/pubmed/25000133>

Even the simple act of giving feelings a name starts to calm them and get them under control: 'Teaching Your Child to Express Emotions, The Centre on the Social and Emotional Foundations for Early Learning' <http://csefel.vanderbilt.edu/familytools/teaching_emotions.pdf>

How to foster children's out-of-school relationships

Benson, Dr Peter Sparks: *How Parents Can Ignite the Hidden Strengths of Teenagers* (Jossey-Bass, 2008)

Scientists have found that hugging for twenty seconds is enough to boost levels of the feel-good hormone oxytocin for hours afterwards: Uvnas-Moberg K., Petersson M. 'Oxytocin, A Mediator of Anti-Stress, Well-Being, Social Interaction, Growth and Healing' *Psychosom Med Psychotherapy* (2005) <https://articles.mercola.com/sites/articles/archive/2017/05/20/hug-benefits.asp>

How to help a child who says: 'Nobody likes me'

Humour can be taught by parents in the home: Sterling Honig, Alice 'Humor Development in Young Children' (*Research in Review*, 1988) <https://www.researchgate.net/publication/234687359_RESEARCH_IN_REVIEW_Humor_Development_in_Young_Children>

Teach children a growth mind-set: Dweck, Carol Mindset: *How You Can Fulfill Your Potential* (Robinson, 2012)

If you have drifted apart

'A slower day is not coming.' Parsons, Rob *The Sixty Minute Family: An Hour To Transform Your Relationships For Ever* (Lion, 2010)

To reclaim your closeness with your child, psychologist Oliver James recommends a technique called 'love bombing': James, Oliver *Love Bombing: Reset Your Child's Emotional Thermostat* (Karnac Books, 2012)

PART FOUR – HOW TO HELP YOUR CHILD HANDLE SOME OF THE MOST COMMON FRIENDSHIP PROBLEMS

Relational aggression between girls

'Unlike boys who tend to bully acquaintances or strangers, girls frequently attack between tightly knit networks of friends, making aggression harder to identify and intensifying the damage to targets: Simmons, Rachel *Odd Girl Out* (Mariner Books, 2011)

Forty-eight per cent of students are regularly exposed to relational aggression: The Ophelia Project <www.opheliaproject.org>

Common reasons why friendships fracture

There are three signs that a friend wants to end a friendship: 'Why Ending a Friendship Can be Worse Than a Break-up' *Time magazine* (24 September, 2018) <http://time.com/5402304/friendship-breakups-worse-romantic/m>

So when should you get involved...?

In Japan pre-schoolers are expected to resolve their own conflicts: Tobin, Joseph *Preschool in Three Cultures Revisited: China, Japan, and the United States* (University of Chicago Press, 2011)

How to help children navigate social media

Half of teens now feel 'addicted' to their mobile devices: 'Common Sense Media Has Found That Half of Teens Now Feel "Addicted' to Their Mobile Devices' (May 2016) <https://www.commonsensemedia.org/about-us/news/press-releases/new-report-finds-teens-feel-addicted-to-their-phones-causing-tension-at>

The sweet spot appears to be allowing them to use social media for up to an hour a day: <http://www.psychology.sdsu.edu/sdsu-psychology-professor-jean-twenge-new-book-igen/>

The more time 14-year-olds were online the more likely they were to get caught up in cyber-bullying: Lacey, Barbara 'Social Aggression: A Study of Internet Harassment, (Hofstra University, 2007) <https://www.learntechlib.org/p/123761/>

British children spend more time on the internet than anyone else in the world: based on the OECD's Programme for International Student Assessment (Pisa) tests, which surveyed 540,000 pupils aged 15 from around the world (April 2017) <https://www.telegraph.co.uk/education/2017/04/19/british-children-spend-time-internet-almost-every-developed/>

Many of the world's biggest technology gurus have now said they don't allow their children to use devices without strict parameters: 'Ex-Facebook President Sean Parker: Site Made to Exploit Human

"Vulnerability"' <https://www.theguardian.com/technology/2017/nov/09/facebook-sean-parker-vulnerability-brain-psychology>

Teenagers who spend five or more hours a day on electronic devices are 71 per cent more likely to have a risk factor for suicide: Twenge, Jean 'Increases in depressive symptoms, suicide-related outcomes, and suicide rates among us adolescents after 2010 and links to increased new media screen time' *Clinical Psychological Science* (2017)

Young people who use phones too much are also 52 per cent more likely to sleep less than seven hours a night: Twenge, Jean 'Decreases in self-reported sleep duration among US adolescents 2009–2015 and association with new media screen time, *Sleep Medicine* (2017) <https://www.sleep-journal.com/article/S1389-9457(17)30350-7/fulltext>

What if you think your child is being bullied?

Children who are bullied at six are significantly more likely to still be victims at the age of ten: 'Who escapes or remains a victim of bullying in primary school?' Wolke, Dieter, Woods, Sarah, Samara, Muthanna, *British Journal of Developmental Psychology* (2010)

Early intervention is important because entrenched bullying can cause high levels of isolation, distress and anxiety: Vernberg E. M., Biggs B. K. *Preventing and Treating Bullying and Victimization* (Oxford University Press, 2010) <https://www.childrensmn.org/images/advocacy/bullying/bullyingwhitepaper_01q_final_web.pdf>

What if it's your child being mean?

Studies by the University of Norway have highlighted several factors in the home that can lead a child to bully: Olweus, Dan, 'Bully/

victim problems in school: Facts and intervention' *European Journal of Psychology of Education* (Springer 1997)

Olweus, D., *Bullying at School: What We Know and What We Can Do* (Wiley-Blackwell, 1993)

How teachers can help

The prevalence of passive aggressive behaviour: Leff, Stephen S., Evian Waasdorp, Tracey, Paskewich, Brooke, Lakin Gullan, Rebecca, Jawad, Abbas F. Paquette MacEvoy, Julie, Feinberg, Betsy E. and Power, Thomas J. 'The Preventing Relational Aggression in Schools Everyday Program: A Preliminary Evaluation of Acceptability and Impact' *School Psychology Review* (2010) <https://www.ncbi.nlm.nih.gov/pmc/articles/PMC3113534/>

Students feel less safe in schools in which relational aggression is frequent: Kuppens, Grietens, Onghena, Michiels and Subramanian 'Individual and Classroom Variables Associated with Relational Aggression in Elementary-School Aged Children: A Multilevel Analysis' *Journal of School Psychology* (2008)

Seventy-seven per cent of the PE students said as result that they did not tell their physical education teacher when they were bullied in these lessons: <https://www.yorksj.ac.uk/media/content-assets/schools/sport/documents/Bullying-in-School-Sport---Final.pdf>

'Bullying is still rife in schools. Here's how teachers can tackle it.' Elizabeth Nassem, researcher at Birmingham City University's Centre for the Study of Practice and Culture in Education (January 2018) <https://www.theguardian.com/teacher-network/2018/jan/17/bullying-is-still-rife-in-schools-heres-how-teachers-can-tackle-it>

When one child bullies another, 54 per cent of witnesses stand by and watch, 21 per cent imitate and only 25 per cent try to stop it: Thornberg, Robert, Tenenbaum, Laura, Varjas, Kris, Meyers, Joel, Jungert, Tomas and Vanegas, Gina 'Bystander Motivation in Bullying Incidents: To Intervene or Not to Intervene?' *The Western Journal of Emergency Medicine* (2012) <https://www.ncbi.nlm.nih.gov/pmc/articles/PMC3415829/>

INTERNET RESOURCES

Relational aggression:
www.opheliaproject.org
www.youtube.com/user/TheOpheliaProjectPA

Bullying:
www.bullying.co.uk
www.signewhitson.com
www.kidscape.org.uk

Social Media:
www.commonsensemedia.org

Improving social skills:
www.additudemag.com
www.socialthinking.com

General parenting advice:
www.kidsinthehouse.com
www.calmerparenting.co.uk
www.ahaparenting.com

NOTES

Have you enjoyed this book?

If so, why not write a review on your favourite website?
If you're interested in finding out more about our books,
find us on Facebook at **Summersdale Publishers** and
follow us on Twitter at **@Summersdale**.

Thanks very much for buying this Summersdale book.

www.summersdale.com